Accommodating Diversity

Accommodating Diversity

National Policies That Prevent Conflict

Irwin Deutscher

LEXINGTON BOOKS
Lanham • Boulder • New York • Oxford

LEXINGTON BOOKS

Published in the United States of America
by Lexington Books
A Member of the Rowman & Littlefield Publishing Group
4720 Boston Way, Lanham, Maryland 20706

PO Box 317
Oxford
OX2 9RU, UK

British Library Cataloguing in Publication Information Available

Library of Congress Cataloging-in-Publication Data

Deutscher, Irwin, 1923-
  Accommodating diversity : national policies that prevent ethnic
  conflict / Irwin Deutscher.
    p. cm.
  Includes index.
  ISBN 0-7391-0457-8 (alk. paper)
  1. Ethnic conflict—Prevention. 2. Multiculturalism. 3. Ethnic
  groups—Government policy. 4. Minorities—Government policy. I. Title.

HM1121 .D48 2002
305.8—dc21   2002010040

Printed in the United States of America

♾™ The paper used in this publication meets the minimum requirements of American
National Standard for Information Sciences—Permanence of Paper for Printed Library
Materials, ANSI/NISO Z39.48–1992.

Contents

Foreword

The world is in transition. But then it always has been and always will be. The transient character of social arrangements is made evident in this wide-ranging, lucidly written book. Irwin Deutscher focuses on what may appear to be a particularly stable element of social life: ethnicities, including those popularly called races. However, he demonstrates the fluidity, complexity, and situational nature of even these groupings. He does so by a kaleidoscopic view of social interactions in various times and places around the world.

Ethnic categories constantly undergo changes as the categories shift and as their meanings are modified. Deutscher vividly illustrates the variability of these categories, pointing out how they are socially constructed and reconstructed. He does so by combining information from newspaper stories, classic and contemporary social theories, empirical research findings, and personal encounters. The fluidity of ethnic and so-called racial categories and identities is due to the reality that everyone has multiple identities. How they are joined together and their relative salience depends greatly on the circumstances in which each person lives, and those circumstances keep changing. The circumstances change as a result of large-scale trends and shattering events, and also as each person moves from place to place and moves through a life course.

Of course, this multiplicity and fluidity of identities mean that some people may be aroused and mobilized against some other people by everyday relationships and family accounts, and by xenophobic exhortations by government officials, intellectuals, and ambitious political or religious leaders. At times, members of a group may hold particularly nasty views of another people, even regarding them as not fully human. They also may believe themselves to be inherently and forever superior to those others or to have been oppressed and victimized by them.

Indeed, much of the recent attention to ethnicities has emphasized the antagonistic quality of interethnic relations and the murderous fights between members of different ethnic groups. These horrific conflicts seem to have been particularly evident in the post-cold war world, with a sharp spike in violent conflicts between communal groups for a few years. Fights between ethnic, religious, and other communal groups flared as countries' authoritarian regimes were ended and political borders were changed.

In many cases, however, societal transitions were accomplished with little or no violence and by negotiated accommodations. After all, the very fluidity of communal identities and structures means that destructive relations and conflicts can be transformed. Old identities can be reformulated and new ones take on prominence. In South Africa, the meaning of being South African and its new significance was an important part of South Africa's negotiated restructuring.

Deutscher discusses many policies that have helped people of different ethnicities live side by side without destructive conflict. These include various forms of assimilation, pluralism, partition, enclaves, and reconciliation. These diverse policies are based on particular sets of ideas and ideologies relating to nationalism, religious beliefs, notions of racism, and conceptions of democracy. These ideas have powerful effects on the choice and implementation of policies regarding interethnic relations. The policies also are shaped by values, as well as by beliefs and evidence about the consequences of different policies.

Deutscher is clear about the evidence he brings to bear and about his values as he examines diverse policies of interethnic accommodations. He particularly explores the implications of the empirical generalization that pluralist policies are an effective way to bring about assimilation. On the other hand, imposed assimilationist policies often backfire.

Deutscher wisely points out that no policy is permanent and none is perfect; how well and for how long they are effective depends on many conditions. These are remarkably sensible observations, remarkable because many people prefer to propose one or another panacea that is supposed to be the solution for all kinds of interethnic conflicts in all kinds of circumstances.

Personally, growing up on Chicago in the 1930s as a child of immigrant parents, I have experienced the pressures and embarrassments resulting from even the moderate American melting pot approach to assimilation. I have also seen considerable changes since then in the conception of what America is and what an American looks like. The contemporary pluralist or multicultural approach is comfortable for greater varieties of people, even as some people react against it. The growing tolerance provides more and more people the opportunity to assimilate into a culture and society that is itself increasingly an amalgam of growing diversity.

There may be a tendency in any society toward assimilation in the long run, particularly if diversity is encouraged, as Deutscher argues. Indeed, in the increasingly integrated world, powerful forces foster increasing similarity and mutual assimilation. Yet, at the same time many people react against the homogenizing trends of globalization, extolling their particular re-creations of past traditions. Increasingly, people of diverse communal identities and practices interact and are compelled to live together, providing more mutual understanding but also more grounds for conflict.

Differences in values and interests will never cease to exist in the world or in a society. So norms and practices of democratic tolerance will forever be relevant and useful. In addition, legitimate institutionalized ways of contending about such differences will also be useful. Democratic systems frequently provide just such ways of nonviolently contending and of engaging in conflict constructively.

One final point should be mentioned. This book is a pleasure to read. Deutscher has been around and has read widely. He has thought hard about one of the most challenging and distressing aspect of human relations and he shares his reflections forthrightly and without pretentiousness. The result, perhaps surprisingly, is hopeful. As he says, the story he tells has a happy ending. I think he provides sensible ideas about how destructive interethnic relations have been overcome, pointing the way to transforming those that have not yet been surmounted

Louis Kriesberg

Preface

This book is a kind of intellectual biography of the past dozen years of my life. It is a record of a search for ideas and conclusions about what I believe to be the most critical issue of our times: the facts about race and ethnicity in the contemporary world. I do not consider myself an expert on these matters. In fact, there may be no experts. I am not, however, the only one who thinks it is an important issue. Many other people do, too, sometimes for what may be the wrong reasons. I had been retired for several years when I began this pursuit. Having spent over a decade pondering these things, I want to share my thoughts with readers in the hope that they will find them useful.

This is a "cut-and-paste" book. There is little here that is not already known. I have pieced together these bits of known facts in a manner which I hope makes them more generally accessible and useful. These are not mere curiosities of history and social life. There is a coherence to them that needs to be recognized. I am appalled, for example, at the lack of public awareness of the Swedish Home Language Act and the Ghanaian Chieftaincy Act, both of which were passed in the 1970s and both of which evidence considerable success in dealing with minorities under very different conditions. I like to think that this process of putting known things together is creative. By recalling them, realigning them, reorganizing them, and spelling out how they might be useful, something different is created.

Since my intent was to compare different times and places in order to determine what kinds of policies might be helpful in other times and places, I naively sought out comparative literature in the social sciences. The effort was ill fated largely because there is so little truly comparative research. There are many edited collections with different authors writing about different places but rarely do they provide any comparative analysis. Among the exceptions is Kinloch's *The Comparative Understanding of Intergroup Relations: A Worldwide Analysis.*[1] As it turned out, this book was not useful for my purposes although that hardly diminishes its authenticity as a comparative study.

Some titles seem deliberately misleading, and thus the book is a disappointment. For example, Sandole's *Capturing the Complexity of Conflict: Dealing With Violent Ethnic Conflicts of the Post-Cold War Era*,[2] neither captures the complexity nor deals with ethnic conflicts. It is rather an analysis of 1960's data. The research was conducted in the psychology laboratory with American college sophomores as subjects. The author claims to have generated a theory which explains ethnic conflict in the twenty-first century. I have serious reservations about that.

Nevertheless, there is an abundance of data available— too much for any one person to digest. Although much of that data is provided by scholars in anthropology, sociology, international relations, conflict resolution, policy studies, and political science, I found other materials which were more timely, sometimes more comparative, and which reflected empirical analysis and descriptions. It was my local newspaper which provided most of that, and in chapter 6 I try to rationalize the use of this secondary data. When I did run across work which suggested how intergroup conflicts might be resolved worldwide, it was usually disappointing. For example, I discovered a book with the subtitle, *Stories of Hope in a World of Conflict*.[3] This, I thought, is exactly what I am looking for.

But as fascinating and hopeful as the anecdotes in that volume are, they turn out to be no more than a continuation of the work of a devoted Swiss-based movement, "Moral Re-Armament," founded in the 1930s by the American clergyman Frank Buchman. This group continues its valiant attempt to change the hearts and minds of individuals as a route toward changing the world. I applaud their effort and wish them well, but it is not closely related to the effort this book makes. This book seeks national policies which constrain *groups* to behave better than they might otherwise. It makes little difference what happens to hearts and minds. It is collective behavior that is our focus.

I did not write this book for my colleagues. They already know or should know most of what is in it. I wrote it for members of the general public who are concerned about ethnic group relations and the violence which often emerges from those relations. Early in the book, I will argue that the ideas of race and ethnicity became prominent as a part of the European colonial expansion beginning in the sixteenth century. Since that time it has become one of the few universal social processes. People all over the world do harm to one another on the basis of their presumed ethnicity.

The book, however, is not a litany of the terror inflicted on minority groups by dominant ones. Some of that is discussed as necessary background in part 1. The heart of the book is a set of modest proposals suggesting that dominant predators and minority prey is not a necessary relationship between two or more ethnic groups. People can get along, and evidence indicates that under certain conditions they do. This little set of proposals can surely be enlarged by students of history and intergroup relations. I hope that their major criticism is my failure to identify other effective policies and that they will do so. The more we are made conscious of successful devices, the more likely they may be considered when crises appear imminent. My gauge of the success of the book will be the extent to which it helps to raise consciousness about the issues it addresses and the solutions which are possible.

One of the few truly comparative analyses of intergroup relations appeared nearly a half century ago as a textbook. In 1965 Tomatsu Shibutani and Kian M. Kwan published *Ethnic Stratification*.[4] It delved into historical antecedents of the problem (in the Roman Empire, for example) as well as international ethnic relations (in China, for example). Their work was in the tradition of Robert E. Park, a nineteenth-century journalist who was to become one of the founders of American sociology. This book is designed more as a "self-help" book for the troubled corners of the contemporary world. Yet, it shares with Shibutani and Kwan a historical and international perspective and ultimately the tradition of Robert E. Park.

Park described sociology as a quest for "the big news."[5] During his years as a newsman, he had pursued his particular stories wherever and whenever they occurred. As a sociologist Park asked what lay behind these stories which could inform us on human behavior and social processes in a more general way. Much of this book is based on particular stories in the contemporary press. The rationale for that is found in chapter 6. The question addressed here is, is there "big news" which can provide useful insights to other peoples in other places at other times?

Park and his colleagues were certain that assimilation is inevitable when dominant and minority groups cohabit.[6] That is an unlikely and perhaps politically untenable conclusion to reach in the ethos of the early twenty-first century. Yet it is my unexpected and unintended conclusion on weighing the stories and the evidence that follow. Another conclusion which emerges as the book progresses is that there are remnants of twentieth-century international ideology which are dysfunctional. They have no place in the twenty-first century where national chauvinism and eventually nationalism itself are increasingly subject to world disapproval.[7]

First, there is the notion of national sovereignty. Even the United Nations is gradually coming to recognize that human rights and international well-being may well require interference in the internal affairs of nation-states who pose a threat to their own citizens or their neighboring states. Although late in coming and of limited effectiveness, interventions in Bosnia and Kosovo reflect this new ideology. The traditional prohibitions in international relations against dividing existing states into new states and of readjusting borders must also be questioned under some conditions—as tenable as it may remain under others. This unfashionable solution to potential intergroup violence is discussed in chapter 10 with the division of Czechoslovakia serving as the prime positive example.

The third shift in ideology is the increasing realization that determination of national policy in terms of "national interest"—best illustrated by the Kissinger policy during and following the Vietnam war—is not only lacking in humanity but is hardly in the best interest of anyone. William F. Schulz's aptly titled *In Our Own Best Interest*[8] documents this shift persuasively. The national interests of a nation no longer can be defined solely in terms of material interests, such as oil or military alliances. Whether in the Balkans, Central Africa, Southeast Asia, or the Middle East, acts of brutal violence by a dominant group against minority peoples are a threat to the well-being of all of us.

The world has not behaved well in recent years. In fact the *World Disasters Report 1995*, issued jointly by the International Red Cross and Red Crescent societies, states flatly that "Today there are hardly any *natural* disasters." The report mentions fifty-six internal wars across the world at that time.[9] Samantha Power's "Bystanders to Genocide" informs us that "In the course of a hundred days in 1994 the Hutu government of Rwanda and its extremist allies very nearly succeeded in exterminating the country's Tutsi minority."[10] All of this in spite of the heroic efforts of the commander of UN forces in Rwanda, Canadian general Romeo Dallaire. And all of this with the complicity of the United States and the rest of the world.

Power reports that the U.S. government not only knew about the genocide early on and failed to intervene, but also led the effort to remove most UN peacekeepers, and blocked any authorization of UN reinforcements. This was during the Clinton administration. George W. Bush (prior to the attacks on New York City and Washington, D.C.), made it clear that this was a bipartisan policy. Power quotes Bush in January 2000 as saying, "I don't like Genocide, but I would not commit our troops."[10]

In spite of traditional U.S. policy, it behooves those organizations or nations with the power to put a stop to it, to move quickly to end efforts by one ethnic entity to remove or annihilate another. It is in our national interest to do so. The heart of this volume is the description in part 2 of five different national policies which are known to have successfully avoided the ultimate in inhumanity, when ethnic groups do violence to one another—when they become predator and prey.

Notes

1. Graham C. Kinloch, *The Comparative Understanding of Intergroup Relations: A Worldwide Analysis* (Boulder, Colo.: Westview Press, 1999).

2. Dennis J. D. Sandole, *Capturing the Complexity of Conflict: Dealing With Violent Ehnic Conflicts of the Post-Cold War Era* (London: Pinter, 1999).

3. Michael Henderson, *The Forgiveness Factor: Stories of Hope in a World of Conflict* (London: Grosvenor Books, 1996).

4. Tomatsu Shibutani and Kian M. Kwan, *Ethnic Stratification: A Comparative Approach* (New York: Macmillan, 1965).

5. Robert E. Park, "News as a Form of Knowledge: A Chapter in the Sociology of Knowledge," *American Journal of Sociology* 45 (1940): 669-86. In this sense, journalists

do occasionally become sociologists (see chapter 6).

6. Much of Park's work can be found in Everette C. Hughes, et. al., eds., *Race and Culture: The Collected Papers of Robert Ezra Park* (Glencoe, Ill.: The Free Press, 1950). For a concise explicit statement of Park's position on the inevitability of assimilation, see the discussion of Louis Wirth in chapter 13 below. The source of that material is Louis Wirth, "The Problem of Minority Groups" in, *Louis Wirth on Cities and Social Life*, ed. Albert J. Riess Jr.(Chicago, Ill.: The University of Chicago Press, 1964), 244-69.

7. The world, including America's closest allies, reacted with alarm to the sometimes hysterical U.S. response to the 2001 attack on New York and Washington. In the jingoism that followed, Americans were threatened with the loss of civil liberties, and the president announced his intention of pursuing military action anywhere in the world with or without the approval of his allies. A few months later the president again offended the whole world by unilaterally creating new trade barriers on the importation of steel.

8. William F. Schulz, *In Our Own Best Interest* (Boston: Beacon Press, 2001).

9. Sanjay Suri, "Political Violence Primary Cause of Global Catastrophies, Says Report," *The Statesman* (15 May 1995), 9.

10. Samantha Power, "Bystanders to Genocide," *The Atlantic* (September, 2001), www.theatlantic.com/issues/2001/09/power.htm 2-3.

11. Power, "Bystanders," 37.

Acknowledgments

I could not have persevered without the encouragement of those who made me feel less lonesome in pursuing this work while isolated from colleagues. Verda, my partner for more than a half century, was not only patient with my preoccupation for over a decade, but was the best of company on many of my trips abroad. My daughter Martha fed me relevant literature while struggling with her own work in such places as Lusaka, Sarajevo, and Foggy Bottom.

The late Adam Podgorecki, banished to Canada by the Polish communist regime, which destroyed his distinguished institute, not only provided continuing venues to air the work which resulted in this book but also taught me what constituted a truly civilized person.

The Department of Sociology at the University of Akron provided continuous support for my work, up to and including the publication of this volume. My early research was immensely aided by my Croatian born graduate assistant, Bojan Klima, with his rich knowledge of Balkan history and politics. I am grateful to Richard Gigliotti, Frank Falk, and John Zipp, the three department chairpersons at the University of Akron who patiently tolerated my endless requests for assistance and to Dean Roger Creel who aided and abetted them.

I thank my former colleagues S. M. (Mike) Miller and Louis Kriesberg for assuring me over the years that this was worth doing. Finally, I am grateful to my friend and perennial shipmate, Reece McGee, not only for his insistence that this volume be published but also for the hours he spent reading and editing the manuscript. His advice has made it a better book than it would otherwise have been. None of it, of course, is the fault of any of them. My friend and fellow author, Uncle Sam Deutscher, always makes me feel that whatever I am doing is worthwhile. Perhaps he needs to share the blame.

Part 1

The Problem

Chapter 1

The Beginning: Abe Lincoln in India and a Pair of Hungarians in Ottawa

I am a Jew. . . . If you tickle us, do we not laugh? if you poison us, do we not die? and if you wrong us, shall we not revenge? If we are like you in the rest, we will resemble you in that. . . . The villainy you teach me, I will execute.

—Shylock in *The Merchant of Venice*, Act III, Scene I

On a hot afternoon an Indian graduate student drove me along a very dusty road in West Bengal. It really was hot, but it wasn't really a road. It was the top of a dike that divided rice fields. In March 1989 there was only one kind of automobile in India although it did come in either black or white. At that time, under India's self-sufficiency program only one type of anything was produced in that country and there were few imports. Our destination was a tribal village a few miles ahead. Like many Westerners, I had been surprised to learn of the existence of tribal peoples living in villages in rural India—peoples with their own distinct cultures and languages. They are remnants of the natives who inhabited the subcontinent before the invasions and settlement of the ancestors of those who currently populate and dominate most of that nation.

The tribal village we were heading for was inhabited by a people designated under Indian law as an "ex-criminal tribe." This implies of course that they had at one time been a criminal tribe and, in this instance, that was true. Also in this instance the tribe had not become a criminal tribe until certain land reforms and allocations, similar to the American homesteading acts, had resulted in much of their traditional hunting and gathering lands being deforested and granted to Indian farmers. When tribal people continued their traditional activities on these lands—gathering crops and spearing livestock—they became criminals and many were convicted and jailed as a consequence. At least this is the essence of the tale told to me by the local anthropologists who now worked closely with the police and other authorities to provide the facilities and resources which would help these newly legalized "ex-criminal tribes" to adapt to new Indian conditions while retaining much of their traditional culture. My host, Professor P.K Bhowmick, then chair of the Anthropology Department at the University of Calcutta, spent much of his long career working with and for these peoples (for more about these scheduled tribes see Bhomick and Y.C. Simhadri).[1]

Our concern here is not, however, with tribal peoples in India; it is with tribal peoples in such places as Northern Ireland, Central Africa, the Balkans, and Brazil. The important character in this vignette is the sophisticated graduate student who was guiding our car along the narrow dike. I had been engaged for a number of years in research which evaluated social and educational programs in the United States and I was trying to learn from him how these Indian anthropologists went about evaluating their efforts to assist tribal peoples. Suddenly he turned angrily toward me, allowing the car to veer dangerously close to the edge of the dike, and shouted, "How about Abraham Lincoln and the American melting pot?" I was surprised and shaken both by the direction the car was taking and the sudden intensity of his usually quiet demeanor. As I tried to grasp the significance of his question, we entered the village and I said to him as he stopped the car, "The American melting pot is not fashionable in America this year. Perhaps it will return in time." But this was not to be the end of it. In fact, it is the starting place of the work which I was to undertake during the decade of the 1990sand which this book reports.

Back in Calcutta I met with an advanced doctoral seminar in anthropology. My intense driver was there and was clearly one of the senior and most influential members of the seminar. I was interested in the ethnographic evaluations of tribal villages, which these students were doing for their dissertations, and the pipelines to policy makers, which their professor, P.K. Bhowmick, had developed. They would have none of it. They preferred to exploit my "Americanness" with a discussion of what they viewed as the great American melting pot. They were committed to an Indian assimilationist policy which seemed to them the only way to unify their large, culturally and linguistically diverse nation. They were appalled when I suggested that the American melting pot was no longer fashionable. Nevertheless, I drew on my archaic recollections of Gunnar Myrdal's *American Dilemma*[2] along with other literature of the 1950s and my personal experiences as an activist during the civil rights movement. I tried to explain to them the rise of the new ethnic identities in America. I must confess that several years later I did learn that a few of the leading scholars of ethnic processes such as Hirschman and Alba[3] considered evidence of the American melting pot to be substantial. We shall hear more from them in chapter 13.

As thought-provoking as that seminar was, my interests did not really begin to crystalize until I found myself in Ottawa two months later (May 1989) listening to Connie Delahanty's review of Canada's failing pluralistic minority policy.[4] It was the contrast that struck me! Here were two cases of nations struggling for humane solutions to problems resulting from the existence of national minorities within their borders and they appeared to move in opposite directions: India yearning for unity and Canada basking in its "mosaic." Unfortunately, neither the assimilationist nor the pluralist policy appeared to be succeeding.

The Ottawa conference was convened by the late Adam Podgorecki, Polish expatriate and distinguished lawyer-sociologist. I mention Podgorecki and his conference for several reasons. First his concern, like mine, was a for a sociology which might be of some use. Second, he was sensitive to the "dark side" of a politically valuable sociology—or "sociotechnics" as he called it. There is always a danger that a useful social science can become the tool of immoral people bent on immoral purposes. Third, the accidental timing and the people I met at this conference were to set me on a course which culminated in this book. And finally, during the following decade Podgorecki continued to provide venues in which I could air the ideas and the facts I will review for you.

Podgorecki and his sociotechnics are touched upon again in chapter 9. For those who are curious, I have tried to describe sociotechnics in some detail elsewhere.[5] What is important is that history was about to provide the final catalyst for me. At the very moment of the Ottawa conference bits of souvenir barbed wire were being sold in Budapest. The Iron Curtain had begun to crumble. Poland removed its communist leadership and one by one the authoritarian regimes of Eastern Europe fell apart to be replaced, hopefully, by democratic governments. By the spring of 1990 even Albania was seeking to establish relations with the rest of the world. That summer East Germany disappeared from the map of Europe.

At a coffee break, I chatted with two young Hungarian participants. I expected them to be elated with recent events at home. I knew that they were opposed to their communist government but to my surprise I discovered that they had reservations about its dissolution. Their explanation was simple enough: "We are Jews," they said. Their concern, it turned out, was with some of the possible consequences of a peasant populist movement. They anticipated a resurgence of religion, nationalism, and antiminority feelings such as anti-Semitism, all of which had been suppressed under the authoritarian communist regime.

Evidence of such phenomena, not only in Hungary but throughout Eastern Europe and in the Soviet Union as well, became increasingly apparent in the months that followed. The Baltic states provide a purely nationalistic instance, while the conflict between Azerbaijanis and Armenians has strong religious undertones. A downside to democratization began to appear. On the other hand it also seemed that democracy had improved conditions for some minorities, such as ethnic Turks in Bulgaria and ethnic Hungarians in Romania. At any rate it became clear to me that the unintended consequences of this new phase in world history deserved attention. As a sociologist, I had devoted my career to various aspects of intergroup relations, always studiously avoiding any analysis of race relations in my own country. This may seem cowardly, but I prefer to think otherwise. I confess that this is a matter in which I have always had great interest in spite of my failure to address it professionally. It seemed to me that in my country, ethnic and especially racial equality was an issue of morality and politics. It had nothing to do with scientific research, since no matter what the findings of studies comparing, say, African Americans and European Americans, all people in my country were supposed to be equal in the eyes of the law. Why would I engage in research when I could not take its findings seriously?

These were matters which should have been settled in the courts and not in scientific journals. When they were not settled in the courts, then, beginning in 1950, my wife and I (and later our daughters) took to the streets engaging in sit-ins and demonstrations and marches to protest the injustice. That seemed more appropriate than studying race relations. I was twice arrested and jailed during those turbulent times. I remain unable to consider American race relations with any degree of scientific detachment. What I began to realize during the seminar in Calcutta was that I might learn more about my own nation's racial problems if I could better understand how other nations deal with these issues.

A final personal vignette will complete my weaving between biography and history. In 1966 I had found myself on a stage at Syracuse University attempting to defend Martin Luther King's unpopular dream calling for an erosion of racial distinctions as all peoples were assimilated into one people. My principal opponent was an angry and articulate Stokely Carmichael (later, Kwame Toure) proclaiming the dogma of "Black is beautiful." There was a profound truth to Carmichael's arguments and the audience, both black and white, were clearly with him. Even I, sitting with my lonely and archaic assimilationist notions, felt that truth and faltered in the dream I shared with King. I was unnerved by the knowledge that as long as one group defines itself as collectively "different" from another group, that difference will become an invidious one.

I experienced a similar feeling while working on educational issues with young radical Native Americans who demanded for their small isolated tribes a return to their own languages and cultures. How, I wondered, could Cherokee children who were educated in the Cherokee language about Cherokee things hope to prosper in an industrial society dominated by English-speaking whites? Nevertheless, Carmichael was a pioneer in a movement that brought about a resurgent pride of ancestry and culture among many American ethnic groups.

I will discuss these new ethnic identities in chapters 4 and 5. The reader will be reminded of Kwame Toure and the Cherokees in chapter 4, where the emphasis is more historical and less biographic. For the moment, it seemed to me that both Toure and the Cherokees warned that, if it ever had existed, the American melting pot was no longer melting. We were, as Glazer and Moynihan put it, "beyond the melting pot."[6] And there I let the matter drop—until it surfaced again in Calcutta in March 1989. Had I misinformed those dedicated Indian students when I suggested that the melting pot was not currently fashionable in America? But first, let us get on with the cue provided by the pair of Hungarian Jews in Ottawa. Could there be a downside to democracy?

Notes

1. P. K. Bhowmick, *The Lodhas of West Bengal* (Bidisa Midnapur, West Bengal: Rarh Samskrita Sangrahalaya, 1963) and Y. C. Simhadri, *Ex-Criminal Tribes of India* (New Delhi: National Publishing House, 1979).

2. Gunnar Myrdal, with the assistance of Richard Sterner and Arnold Rose, *An American Dilemma: The Negro Problem and Modern Democracy* (New York: Harper and Brothers, 1944).

3. I discovered that the unfashionable assimilationist position still lurked in American sociology when I ran across Charles Hirschman's "What Happened to the White Ethnics?" *Contemporary Sociology,* 20, no. 2 (March 1991): 180-83.

4. Connie Delahanty, "Multiculturalism: Policy or Myth?" (paper presented at the annual meeting of the Society for Applied Sociology, Cincinnati, Ohio, November 1990).

5. See my "Reflections on the Ottawa Papers," in *Dilemmas of Effective Social Action,* ed. Jerzy Kubin (Warsaw: Polish Sociological Association, 1990), 299-306, and Socio-Technics: What's That?" *Journal of Applied Sociology* 6 (1989): 1-8.

6. Nathan Glazer and Daniel Patrick Moynihan, *Beyond the Melting Pot: The Negroes, Puerto Ricans, Jews, Italians, and Irish of New York City* (Cambridge, Mass.: M.I.T. Press, 1963).

Chapter 2

Democracy and Its Downside

Democracy without constitutional liberalism is not simply inadequate, but dangerous, bringing with it the erosion of liberty, the abuse of power, ethnic divisions, and even war.

> —Stephen S. Rosenfeld, "Democracy: The Down side"
> *The Washington Post,* 5 December 1997, 27(A)

When the plane landed in Prague I found a city in the throes of change. Although the monument on Wenceslas Square was heaped with fresh flowers celebrating the end of the Soviet occupation, the shops still exhibited only the limited supplies of drab Soviet style clothing and the hotels continued to be staffed by uncaring and inattentive *apparatchniks.* What was I doing in Prague in the spring of 1990 at the height of the "Velvet Revolution"? I was on my way to Bratislava.Taking my cue from the two Hungarians I had spoken with over coffee in Ottawa, I began to consider the possibility of negative consequences of the end of communism in Eastern Europe.

The Ottawa group met again in the spring of 1990 in Bratislava—a city I had never heard of. I found it on the map— a day long bus ride from Prague. It would not be long before it became the capital of the new state of Slovakia. (I will consider that phenomenon in chapter 10.) Czechoslovakia had only recently shed its Soviet masters and the streets of Prague were a mixture of heady celebration and panicky concern. What must it be like to suspect that your money is no longer worth anything? Everywhere my wife and I went we were accosted by people wanting to buy dollars—hotel maids, cab drivers, waiters, pedestrians. But by and large it was a time of euphoria.

The Iron Curtain had just collapsed and most authoritarian regimes in Eastern Europe had gone with it. When the bus to Bratislava paralleled the Danube River, recently abandoned watch towers, designed to confound any flight to freedom by Czechoslovakian citizens, continued to guard the border. But now the ferryboats had begun to run frequently and freely between Bratislava and nearby Vienna. The last city to appear on the horizon on the other side of the bus was Brno, whose skyline was an obtrusive range of monotonous grey high rise apartments—the standard Eastern European provision for housing the masses. To my relief, Bratislava had the appearance of a quaint medieval river town. On the very day that President Havel was inaugurated to the joy of the populace, I delivered my address to an audience composed of about one-half international visitors and one-half local intellectuals and scholars.

The inauguration was a memorable event for a people relishing a long sought freedom from foreign oppression. For me it was not so memorable. In an exercise of incredibly poor timing I chose to deliver an essay on the potential negative consequences of the newly emerging era. I concentrated on the downside of democracy and it is hardly remarkable that no one paid attention. At the very least it was tactless for me to suggest that without the Soviet lid on religious and ethnic violence, there was a high probability that such violence would accompany the new wave of nationalism in Eastern Europe and in the states of the former Soviet Union. Although the potential for interethnic violence was my major concern, I included a number of other elements of the downside of democracy. This chapter closely follows that 1990 essay.

In the euphoria of freedom from authoritarian constraints, first, Eastern European countries and, then, the Soviet republics themselves learned that "democracy," however defined, unmasks certain problems which were suppressed under totalitarian regimes. Civil strife in the former Yugoslavia provides the most dramatic example. The lesson to be learned from this recent history is that the removal of authoritarian dictatorships carries consequences which were not intended. Emerging democracies may avoid such unintended consequences if they can anticipate them. I identify a set of such consequences of democratization in this chapter and each is discussed briefly. It is suggested that even such prototype democracies as Great Britain and the United States fall far short of the political and economic utopia toward which most contemporary nations strain.

There is often a false equation between democracy and a free market economy when in fact there is little relationship between the two: Barber[1] reminds us that the free market flourished in junta-run Chile, in military-governed Taiwan and Korea, and, earlier, in a variety of autocratic European empires as well as their colonial possessions. The importance of considering such matters is underscored by the American secretary of state's announcement in 1993 that he fully backed the campaign commitments by President Clinton to make promotion of democracy a central tenet of U.S. foreign policy. In fact the Clinton administration pursued this policy until the very end. In the spring of 2000 the next secretary of state designated four "key democracies" that would be the focus of U.S. aid: Nigeria, Colombia, Indonesia, and the Ukraine.[2]

The Fragility of Democracy

It is not always clear what is intended by the term "democratization," other than as a general description of the alternatives people saw to their formerly totalitarian and oppressive regimes, which began to crumble in Eastern Europe in 1989. Some view it as primarily a guarantee of the kinds of human rights embodied in the U. S. Bill of Rights: freedom to speak and worship as one pleases without reprisal, freedom to gather together at will, freedom from unequal treatment by police, access to the machinery of justice, freedom of movement, and similar personal guarantees and protection from injustice. In 1991, for example, the new president of Ethiopia announced that the most important thing about democracy is "that people can be free to talk without looking back over their shoulders."[3]

Political scientists are inclined to define the essence of democracy as a multiparty system embodied in the concept of a loyal opposition. For some it means little more than the casting off of the old system. Thus in their analysis of survey data collected in the early 1990s from citizens of nine former Soviet satellites, Rose and his colleagues define as democrats all those who disapprove of the former communist regime and support whatever replaced it.[4] For many, democracy is confused with a free market economy with its encouragement of private property, entrepreneurship, competition for wealth, and related economic privileges. Rupert quotes a resident of Tashkent, Uzbekistan, "people do not understand what democracy means politically. . . . For them it is a word associated with the prosperity they see in Europe and America— and so they want it."[5] A decade later, commenting on the U.S. State Department's Annual Report on Human Rights, Hoagland lamented "Uzbekistan's failure to move out of the Soviet era and toward modern democracy and free markets."[6]

Pollster Gordon Heald of the Gallup organization reports what appeared, in early 1992, to be an increasing dissatisfaction with democracy in Eastern Europe and Russia. "The most disillusioned," he reports, " are Russians and those who have been free longest—the Poles, Hungarians, and Czechoslovaks." On the other hand, he told reporters, "Hopes of a better life were highest in Albania, whose Stalinist rulers fell in 1991."[7] Conor Cruise O'Brien is not the only writer to have observed that "many of those who are now attracted to democracy, because of its associations with success and economic well-being in the West, may well recoil from it when they find that democracy does not immediately deliver those good things."[8] Unfortunately, as those who live in eastern Germany know, democracy may not only fail to immediately deliver the "good things." It may, in fact deliver some unexpected bad things as well. I will get to those in a moment.

Mercier argues, "How states treat their minorities is a measure of their democracy."[9] I would put it more strongly: *It is my position that the true test of democracy is the manner in which a state treats its minorities.* A republic in which the majority has its way at the expense of other citizens is no democracy at all. Witness the barbarity of "the Terror" following the fall of the Bastille or the more persistent forms of prejudice and discrimination which became institutionalized in America following its Civil War. Hoagland, writing of what he calls "incomplete democracy" sums it up:

> Without the enforceable safeguards and strong institutions needed to protect minority views *and* the national interest against conventional wisdoms and unconventional passions of any voting majority, elections become merely another tool in the hands of the powerful and unscrupulous.[10]

In this sense there have been times in the history of both France and the United States when these republics would have failed a principal test of democracy. De Tocqueville, although a great admirer of America's budding democracy, devoted one chapter of his *Democracy in America* to "The Unlimited Power of the Majority in the United States" and another to the "Tyranny of the Majority in the United States."[11]

These observations are not intended as criticism of Germany, France, or the United States. Rather they are intended to document the fragility of democracy and its sometimes vulnerability to failures and shortfalls. Even the exemplars of contemporary democracy find that democracy requires vigilance if it is to survive either leaders who believe they know what is best for the people, the majority of the people themselves who are frequently intolerant of the rights of minorities, or, even more threatening, a combination of the two. In my own country there are organizations, such as the American Civil Liberties Union, which are designed to protect democracy by providing legal resources on behalf of the rights of unpopular people and unpopular causes. This, of course, sometimes makes such organizations unpopular.

America has a long history of threats to its democratic survival. The 1856 presidential campaign found Millard Fillmore running as a "Know-Nothing" on an anti-Catholic platform. Later in the nineteenth century there were popular riots against "foreigners" which culminated in a Chinese immigrant exclusion act in 1882.[12] Actions taken by industry and government against workers and the organizers of labor unions were equally threatening; the detention of Americans of Japanese descent during the Second World War is a blot on our history nearly as repulsive as slavery; the fearful witch-hunting McCarthy era of the 1950s remains a cautionary memory.

It is not difficult to find evidence for both the fragility of democracy and the constant threat of intolerance. The homes of Americans who were thought to be Iraqis were vandalized and the people terrorized during the patriotic fervor of the Gulf War. In at least one case, the press suggested this was unfortunate because the victims had been "mistaken for Iraqis." They were described by Baker as "victims of cruel error,"[13] implying that had they in fact been of Iraqi descent, the behavior would have been justified. Following the events of September 11, 2001, a resurgent patriotic fervor in the United States led to extensive harassment of people thought to be "Arabs." In January 2002, the Justice Department listed as least nine murders of persons of Middle Eastern descent during that period "as possible hate crimes."[14] This in spite of President Bush's persistent reminders that such acts were intolerable.

The first lesson for aspirants is that democracy is not a thing which, once attained, can be lazily enjoyed. Some third world democracies are well aware of this. India, for example, is engaged in a constant struggle to maintain democracy in the face of conflict among ethnic, linguistic, and religious groups. Conditions in Kashmir are surely as embarrassing to most Indians as the "Know Nothings" and McCarthyites were to most Americans.

A second lesson concerns the assumed inherent economic advantage of capitalism over socialism. In Canada, one of the world's great democracies, half of the population lives in provinces which have freely elected majority socialist parties. Michael Massing reminds us that "unbridled capitalism has fared little better than socialism in the third world. In Asia, the Philippines, a welcome mat for Western capital, has not done much better than nearby Vietnam." He goes on to comment that "In Africa neither Zaire nor Liberia seems a good advertisement for Western-style economics." Finally, he turns to our own hemisphere where "the sprawling shantytowns of Lima, Rio, and Caracas bear squalid witness to the dark underside of capitalist development."[15]

It is my position that issues related to minorities—ethnic, religious, national, or racial—emerge as the most dangerous threat to the process of democratization in nations which have freed themselves from oppressive regimes. I have made no effort to define democracy although I have reported different ways in which others view it. But no matter what precise definition is used, I will argue that one of the truest tests of democracy is the protection afforded to minorities who cannot mobilize sufficient votes to protect themselves. The rest of this book deals with ethnic minorities, but, for the moment let us consider some other kinds of problems that appear to result from democratization.

Some Unintended Consequences of Democratization

How can one anticipate unintended consequences of proposed social actions? The social psychologist Donald Campbell suggests that if we pay close attention to the dire predictions of those who oppose a proposed change, we can identify possible consequences which were not intended.[16] Opponents often make such predictions and sometimes they are correct. An example can be found in a 1988 law passed by the Illinois legislature requiring applicants for a marriage license to be tested for the HIV virus that causes AIDS. The county clerks strongly opposed the law, claiming that it would cause local people to go to neighboring states for their marriages. This was a matter of concern to the county clerks since they receive $15.00 for each marriage license issued. Federal health statistics reveal that these opponents were correct in their dire predictions: marriage rates in Illinois dropped dramatically in 1988 while the rates in neighboring states showed an equally dramatic increase.[17]

An example closer to the theme of this chapter was the effort of a high-ranking Soviet prosecutor to open a criminal case against President Gorbachev. A report by Hiatt reveals that Gorbachev was accused of lawlessness for recognizing the Baltic states—a violation of the 1990 law providing for a transitional period. It was argued that democracy would bring about not only legal nihilism but would endanger Russian ethnics in other republics, and reduce living standards for everyone. Mr. Ilyukhin, the prosecutor who opposed democratization, concluded that these unintended consequences "have brought the whole country into chaos."[18]

Over a decade later nations such as Latvia continued to punish their Russian ethnics with restrictive language laws and denial of citizenship. La Franier believes that it is only the lure of the security of NATO membership and economic benefits of European Union membership that is persuading such new "democracies" to refrain from the denial of human rights to their minorities.[19]

In addition to listening to the critics, one can anticipate the unintended by examining historical instances of similar actions and determining their consequences. Although valuable clues may be learned from the opponents of democracy, it is to recent history that we turn in this chapter to identify a set of possibly unintended consequences of democratization. The rapid democratization of Eastern Europe provides an opportunity to search for such consequences (as Ilyukhin suggested). These are discussed in no particular order other than that it is the last one which is of the greatest importance. The loss of women's rights is not listed as a separate category, since the decline of freedom for women is infused in nearly every type of loss that is considered.

The Breakdown of Social Control

With the collapse of authoritarian control in Eastern Europe, a variety of phenomena, which had been effectively repressed, suddenly appeared: Vice, pornography, prostitution, purse snatching, and mugging, among others, were apparent in nearly every big city of the east. I mentioned earlier my good fortune to be in Prague at the time of Czechoslovakia's "velvet revolution." But along with the euphoria and celebration of freedom, these dark images also surfaced. The demise of the police state means an end of fear of quick and severe reprisal for infractions of the law. The sudden availability of firearms does not help matters. Soviet crime statistics report 7,000 crimes involving firearms in 1990 and "police seized cash and valuables worth 3.5 million rubles from drug dealers and producers."[20]

In his summary of Soviet crime statistics, Varum reports that in 1990 in Moscow there was a 210 percent increase over 1989 in crimes reported to the police. In the first six months of 1990 there was a 140 percent increase in crime rates in Armenia, Georgia, and Lithuania and 150 percent increase in Tajikistan. In the Soviet Union as a whole there was a sharp increase in thefts, robberies, and burglary when 1989 is compared to 1984 (the only decrease reported was in "hooliganism" which presumably was a label used for political trouble makers). According to the Associated Press, crime in Russia continued to rise dramatically through 1992.

The relationship between violent crime and democracy is far from clear. The Population Crisis Committee provides interesting data.[21] They report that in spite of the increases in Eastern Europe, Moscow's rate of seven murders per 100,000 people is far below Mexico City's 27.6 while in places like the Tokyo Metropolitan area (1.4) and Calcutta (1.1), murder is practically nonexistent (Population Crisis Committee). The only clear fact is that with the elimination of totalitarian police powers, there is an immediate increase in many kinds of crime and vice.

The Loss of Social Security

In East Germany, probably the most repressive dictatorship in Europe since the demise of Josef Stalin, every adult had a job in 1989. It was the law! Freed from the yoke of tyranny and now a part of the democratic capitalist state of Germany, eastern Germans, according to official statistics, suffered the phenomenal unemployment rate of 16.2 percent in 1993. Women suffered the most as reported by a poll from the Allensbach Institute.[22]

In the Polish elections of October 1991, the former Communists regained considerable strength at the polls, finishing within a percentage point of the strongest, Solidarity Party. Much of this unexpected gain appears to derive from the Communist's accusation that Solidarity had wrecked social services.[23] At least to some degree, socialist societies have guaranteed their citizens the right not only to employment, but to housing, medical care, education and a pension in later life, but on January 1, 1993, when Czechoslovakia became two countries, free health care was discontinued.[24]

Some democratic countries attempt to maintain such perquisites, but they are not inherent to democracy and are never secure. The conservative government elected in Sweden in mid-1991 threatened to rescind much of the social security Swedes have become accustomed to. The British welfare system was dismantled under Margaret Thatcher and the optimistic programs begun in the United States under Franklin D. Roosevelt during the Great Depression and continued under Lyndon Johnson's hopeful "Great Society" have gradually disintegrated first under Ronald Reagan and later under George Bush and Bill Clinton. Bush threatened to veto all legislation coming from Congress dealing with civil rights, unemployment, medical assistance, environmental control, and education. After early abortive efforts to promote such issues as universal health care, the Clinton administration became increasingly timid. Toward the end of the Clinton administration, emboldened Republicans were proposing to privatize both Social Security and the public school system.

When the yoke of tyranny is removed, much of the security that a paternalistic government provides also falls away. Democracies may or may not be humane in their treatment of those citizens who are less well off than others. The kinds of social security described here are an inherent element of socialist states—even the most vicious of them. In a capitalist democracy they cannot be taken for granted. When a nation moves from any form of socialist economy toward a more capitalist one, its people must be prepared for the possibility that their basic needs will not be routinely met as well as they had been. In 1989 Estonia was the most prosperous of the Soviet Union's fifteen former republics. With the euphoria of freedom rapidly fading, the winter of 1992 found Estonians suffering cruel economic hardship:

> Only children under 4 years of age can receive milk. Many homes are chilly and without hot water, and the government soon may have to evacuate about 200,000 resident—nearly half the capital's population—to wood-heated homes outside the city because it is running out of heating oil.[25]

The Need for the Old Guard to Maintain the Infrastructure

There is in every language a name for them: *functionnaires, apparatchiks, bureaucrats.* The name is generally spoken with contempt and intended to imply a massive network of unnecessary if not incompetent and sometimes corrupt officials whom one encounters in any venture involving government— national or local—and its services. One of the delusions of people freeing themselves from an authoritarian government is that this will also free them from the agents of government who make the wheels of society turn, no matter how slowly.

To remove the well-known and despised bureaucrats at the top of the national hierarchy is a simple matter. But what of all of the local appointees down to the village level who were employed by the state to issue permits, see to it that the utilities worked, the roads were maintained, the mail was delivered, and the trains kept running, along with hundreds of other mechanisms that keep a national infrastructure operating? In Eastern Europe most lower level and local functionaries were party members only because that was required of such job holders.

In the summer of 1990 the Czechs taught the world a lesson when one of Havel's first announcements as prime minister of the new republic was that all citizens had been victims of communism. Although the hated secret police were all dismissed, they were provided with unemployment compensation for sufficient time to search for new jobs. But other communist bureaucrats were kept in their jobs and the country continued to operate. The philosophy espoused by Havel played no small part in the eventual peaceful dissolution of Czechoslovakia into two nations.

Unfortunately, Havel was not to have his way for long. In November of 1991, something referred to locally as "The Hunt" was begun in Czechoslovakia. It resulted from the passage of a "de-communization law that requires all former senior Communist Party officials, party police, and their collaborators to be dismissed or demoted."[26] Havel reluctantly supported the bill, hoping that it could be amended later. By the end of 1991, similar punitive measures designed to seek retribution had been passed in Hungary, Bulgaria, and Poland. The chain of events released by a policy of vengeance is described by the Polish newspaper editor Adam Michnik as reminiscent of the French Revolution:

> This is our Jacobite period. In the beginning they demanded the king's head. Then they wanted his entourage. And then they moved against anyone who had spoken out against the reprisals. It is a road without end. If you punish a hundred, there will always be a thousand more.[27]

At the turn of the twentieth century Max Weber made the distinction between pre-industrial forms of social organization and the kinds of social organization beginning to appear in modern industrialized society. He called the earlier model a charismatic form of organization and the emerging one a bureaucratic form. The complexity of modern industrial society and the modern city was such that it required a new and more complex form of political organization if things were to get done. Weber aptly describes bureaucracy as a sort of necessary evil. He spoke of it as an iron cage in which we will ultimately imprison ourselves.[28] All of that aside, it should be clear that it is not possible for a complex society to dispose of bureaucracy without disposing of its complexity along with it.

For Weber, bureaucracy was rational, efficient, and unfeeling. He didn't care much for it, but he recognized its necessity. In the nineteenth century Weber understood what Havel understood in the twentieth.

> The objective indispensability of the once-existing apparatus, with its peculiar, "impersonal" character, means that the mechanism—in contrast to feudal orders based upon personal piety—is easily made to work for anybody who knows how to gain control over it. A rationally ordered system of officials continues to function smoothly after the enemy has occupied the area: he merely needs to change the top officials. This body of officials continues to operate because it is to the vital interest of everyone concerned.[29]

With democratization and capitalism, what were once simpler, more personal, warmer, informal kinds of societies became rationalized into the kind of impersonal bureaucracy with which all industrialized societies—whether communist or capitalist—have long been familiar.

Freedom from Tyranny Is Not Democracy

As people achieve freedom from what they defined as totalitarian overlords, they are inclined to assume that their political troubles are over. Late-twentieth-century examples provided by Serbia, Romania, and Georgia illustrate the survival of former Communist Party leaders along with their ability to maintain authority while not always adjusting easily to the kinds of freedoms the people expected. Well into the 1990s, in Azerbaijan, Lithuania, Tajikistan, Turkmenistan, and Uzbekistan local Soviet-era Communists maintained the autocratic rule established under the Kremlin. Authoritarian leadership on the right emerged in Hungary, Slovakia, and Croatia.[30] In such cases a new oppressive one-party system replaced an old repressive one-party system.

Iran and Poland illustrate in their own ways how the demise of one kind of oppression may open the door to another. Iran, having freed itself from the control of a local elite established and supported by a foreign power, turned itself into an authoritarian theocracy which persisted throughout the 1990s before moderating. The steps toward freedom made by women under the previous regime were quickly reversed and religious intolerance and persecution became official policy. The death of Khomeini made no difference. Among those executed under Rafsanjani are hundreds of teenage girls and pregnant women. Anderson and Van Atta report that,

> Iranian law allows for the execution of adulterous women by stoning, burning, being thrown off a cliff or having a wall collapsed on them. A United Nations human rights report earlier this year [1991] said Rafsanjani's regime had even established the right of men to kill their wives, sisters and daughters for immorality. For revealing the face she is supposed to keep veiled, an Iranian woman can be beaten with 74 lashes and lose her government job.[31]

Baha'i, the largest religious minority in Iran, bears the brunt of this oppression because of what fundamentalist clerics perceive to be its "dangerous" ideology. The religion of Baha'i obliges its adherents to obey the law, avoid partisan politics, and shun violence. Perhaps most dangerous of all is their belief in the acceptance of all religions. Iran's treatment of the Baha'i is described by Anderson and van Atta as nothing short of "barbaric."

Poland, on the other hand, continues to struggle toward democracy, but it is indeed a struggle. The resurgence of communist strength at the polls is not Poland's only problem. Much of that struggle toward democracy in this almost completely Catholic country is between the Catholic Church (a powerful ally of the Solidarity movement which freed Poland) and the Polish people. Although the Polish theocracy is less powerful than the Iranian one, it nevertheless has succeeded in reversing many of tHe freedoms achieved by women.[32] Previously available birth control information is no longer available and abortion is no longer an option. Polish government surveys conducted in March 1991 showed public support for the church had dropped to 58 percent, down from 83 percent a year earlier.

Oddly enough, in eastern Germany where abortion was a freely exercised choice under the oppressive communist regime, it is increasingly restrictive under the democratic German government. Kova's Hungarian data lead her to conclude that "women are affected by disadvantageous social and economic processes more seriously than are men. Also, the new ways of being entrepreneurs are less available for females."[33] Women do not appear to fare well with democratization. As we have seen, sometimes no one fares well since it is always possible for one set of tyrannies to be replaced by another. The demise of an *Ancien Regime* does not necessarily lead to democracy.

The world watched with joy as one after another of Eastern Europe's communist regimes was toppled by popular demand. But if it was the shipyard workers who freed Poland, it was old line Communists who "freed" Romania. In some cases the new freedom appears to contain the seeds of its own destruction. With Irish history as his source, O'Brien suggests that, with the demise of imposed tyranny in multinational polities, there is a concomitant rise in nationalism and nationalism leads to intolerance:

> And in each nationality that is struggling to emerge, aroused nationalism is intolerant of dissent, especially the dissent of local ethnic minorities: "No free speech for traitors!" was a slogan frequently heard in Ireland in the Twenties and Thirties, in the aftermath of the Irish Civil War. That slogan would be readily intelligible today in Georgia and Azerbaijan, or in Serbia and Croatia [and, with hindsight, Bosnia].[34]

In contemporary Europe, xenophobia is endemic. In Germany it spread like a plague from the newly free east to the forty-year-old model democracy in the west. With increasing migration of peoples in search of political and economic hope—from southern and eastern Europe as well as Africa, the Middle East, and Asia—there is escalating violence by young people and resentment from older ones. Germany, although hardly unique in this respect, is the most dramatic instance because of its official policy of hospitality toward political refugees. The German government is beginning to waver in that increasingly unpopular policy.

Problems of racial intolerance in Europe became so disturbing that the city council of Birmingham (England) hosted a conference in December 1991 sponsored by the Council of Europe, the European Commission, and various British public organizations. These European officials hoped that by sharing their experiences with minority issues, they would be able to learn more about "the development of equality for all."

These have been some of the more readily observable, if unintended, consequences of the process of democratization following the collapse of the Soviet
Union. Examples are abundant in newspaper reports of the period. Our discussion
has drifted inevitably into the final and most important unintended consequence
of democratization—the one forecast by my two Hungarians in Ottawa.

The Revival of Ethnic and National Sentiments

One of the first and perhaps the most potentially devastating lessons the
world learned from the expulsion of communist totalitarian authority from
Eastern European nations was that certain kinds of sentiments can be successfully
suppressed for the better part of a century and yet emerge anew with all of their
former destructiveness. The revival of religion throughout Eastern Europe and
the former Soviet Union was spontaneous and instantaneous when the police
power to repress it dissolved. So too was the revival of traditional national and
ethnic suspicions and animosities. In the spring of 1991 pollster Mark Penn
directed a survey of thousands of randomly selected adults in Hungary, Poland,
and Czechoslovakia. He found that seven out of ten people in those countries
would prefer not having any Gypsies for neighbors:

> Two out of three said that they would not like having Arabs as neighbors. Half
> would prefer that blacks or Asians stayed out of their neighborhood. Just over a
> third of all of those questioned did not want to live next door to Russians, and
> one out of four didn't want Jews as neighbors.[35]

Such sentiments are, of course, not peculiar to emerging democracies. A
Gallop poll conducted only a few months later (October, 1991) showed "that 20
to 30 percent of Austrians hold antisemitic and xenophobic views."[36] Although
31 percent of the Austrians preferred not to have Jews as neighbors, even greater
percentages of them objected to living near Poles, Slovenes, Croats, Serbs, and
Turks. Furthermore, one of five French people would not want their child to
marry a Jew.[37] It is a troublesome commentary on democracy that among former
East German youth and adults "80% were found free of prejudice against Jews,
as opposed to 30% in former West Germany."[38]

It is not my purpose to argue against nationalism or ethnic loyalty, except
when these phenomena lead to people doing harm to other people on the basis of
national origins or ethnicity. As I wrote the first draft of this chapter more than a
decade ago, the press reported Serbian rockets hitting the Croatian capital of
Zagreb (October 8, 1991). This was but the beginning of the horror that was to
follow in Bosnia and ultimately to conclude in Kosovo. Although unrelated to
democratization, a Reuters reporter tells, on this same day, of witnessing the
execution of sixty unarmed Iraqi soldiers by Kurdish rebels. As Shakespeare

observed in the heading to my first chapter, an oppressed minority is capable of exercising all of the savagery it has learned from its oppressors. The third world is no more free of ethnic and national sentiments than is the rest of the world.

One caveat is important. Democratization does not *cause* the undesirable consequences described in this chapter. A picture of Nigeria as it emerged in 1999 from decades of pillage by an authoritarian military government suggests that a new democracy can find such problems already in place:

> The electricity is seldom on in much of West Africa's most populous and richest country. The telephone system routinely crashes. Ethnic and religious strife has killed hundreds in recent months. And the executive and legislative branches of the new democratic government are engaged in bitter verbal warfare that has stymied passage of a national budget.[39]

The Revival of Ethic and National Sentiments

I choose to focus on this issue because I believe it is very likely to occur as a consequence of democratization. The surge of formerly oppressed people toward freedom can pose an immediate threat to that very process. We touched on the fragility of democracy earlier in this chapter. Let us consider now what instruction we can receive from recent history. There is no scarcity of the kinds of little stories from which the "big news" discussed in the preface must be built. In this section I will review the scope and seriousness of national and ethnic conflict which emerged immediately following the collapse of the Iron Curtain in 1990 and into early 1991. This review is based largely on reports in the *Washington Post* which happened to be my home town newspaper at the time.

Some instances are so commonplace and persistent that they are taken for granted by the world. At the time this included the everyday reports of the deadly and violent tribal conflicts in Sri Lanka, the continuing demands of Palestinians for rights in their own country, the seemingly endless conflict in South Africa, not only between blacks and whites but also tribal-based violence among black groups. The enduring war between Catholic and Protestant in Northern Ireland has become so commonplace that it is hardly noted in the daily press. Continuing efforts to keep the Canadian federation from falling apart also belong in this category of the commonplace.

Other instances of such intergroup conflict were so obscure as to be hardly recognizable by most of the world. Although Iraq's treatment of its Kurdish minority is familiar enough, who is familiar with that country's militant repression of its Assyrian minority? We all recognize the persistent religious violence in Kashmir and the ongoing conflict between Pakistan and India in that area, but the violence which resulted in martial law in Hyderabad and clashes between rival ethnic groups in Karachi is less familiar. That conflict is blamed on descendants of Muslem migrants from India following the 1947 partition. They are demanding official recognition as Pakistan's fifth nationality group.

Falling somewhere between these extremes of journalistic notoriety and obscurity is a broad set of widely scattered events which occurred during this short period of history. The Kashmir troubles are one such event as are the ethnic disturbances reported in Kashgar, China's westernmost city, populated mostly by Muslem Uighurs. The government of Liberia collapsed after a long and bloody struggle between two tribal coalitions: the Krahns and Mandingos fighting the Gios and Manos. Turkey's ten million Kurds continue to wage their war for independence, unlike Iraq's Kurds who are fewer in number and ask only for a degree of autonomy within the Iraqi state. More recently, tens of thousands of Muslem women and children have fled from Myanmar (formerly Burma) to neighboring Bangladesh, already one of the poorest countries in the world. They accuse Myanmar's Buddhist military junta of "launching an indiscriminate campaign of violence and intimidation aimed at driving Muslims of the ethnic Rohingya minority out . . . to make room for [ethnic] Buddhist settlers."[40] As pathetic as it may be to consider people seeking refuge in the poverty of Bangladesh, it is not unique. By the first of the following year 60,000 Tajiks had fled their civil war into Afghanistan, where many froze to death.[41]

The former communist controlled countries of Eastern Europe provide a dramatic set of cases. Romania was the only country where the military resisted the rebellious people. At first Rumanians and ethnic Hungarians joined together to overthrow Nicolae Ceausescu who had embarked on a policy of systematically destroying all traces of Hungarian culture in Romania. But Transylvania in the early 1990s is described as a place of fear, tempers, and violent nationalism. One Rumanian writer reminds us that "The miners savage attack on demonstrating students in Bucharest last June 14 and 15 [1990] was well covered in the Western media. . . . But not much was written about the miners gratuitous assault on the Gypsies."[42] In the new "democratic" Romania, ethnic Hungarians, Gypsies, and Germans find themselves constantly under threat.

Yugoslavia consisted of six republics, two autonomous provinces, more than a dozen nationalities, three major religions, and two alphabets. In free elections, both Slovenia and Croatia threw out their communist officials and declared themselves independent states. Slovenia got away with it but it was not so easy for Croatia with its ethnic Serbs, its border with Serbia, a largely Serbian national army, and an expansionist Serbian government, all fighting to prevent Croatian autonomy. Bosnia, with local Serbs and Croats both fighting for most of that region, had little hope for survival without outside help. But the world only watched as it self-destructed. Czechoslovakia and Hungary, both with long standing democratic traditions also had their troubles. Czechs and Slovaks, although without violence, had their extreme nationalists who succeeded in splitting the country in two and ethnic Hungarians, Gypsies, and Jews are unlikely to fare well in Slovakia. The new Hungarian government elected in the spring of 1990 ran on a nationalist platform of "Hungarian-ness" while its defeated opponents had stood for "European-ness." Public anti-Semitic and anti-Gypsy statements surfaced almost immediately.

All of these differences seemed to pale besides the mass of nationality issues confronting the former Soviet Union. There has been a massive exodus of Soviet Jews to Israel and elsewhere. Interviews with some who fled to the New York City area suggest that they suffered nearly all of the consequences of democratization reviewed in this chapter. Orleck's respondents insist that there was nothing left for them in the former Soviet Union. They felt intimidated not only by the resurgence of anti-Semitism but also by the general economic chaos and the rise of violent crime.[43]

I will not review the litany of Soviet republics which have declared their independence from the old union and from Russia. But the fact that the Baltic states became nations again left as many nationality and ethnic issues unsolved as it solved. According to the Estonian government, Russians made up 40 percent of Estonia's population and were a majority in the capital.[44] Latvians too were a minority in their own capital.[45] About a third of the population of Latvia and Estonia was Russian. There are also sizable Polish and German minorities, but the potential problem with Russian ethnics lay in their total isolation from the Baltic peoples. They lived in the cities, worked in former Soviet industries, had their own residential areas, schools, entertainment, etc. These Russian-Balts were more prosperous and better employed than their hosts and very few managed to learn a word of the Baltic languages.

In the early 1990s it was estimated that "One out of every four Soviet citizens—including about 24 million ethnic Russians—live[d] outside their titular republic."[46] Because of the settlement policy instituted by Stalin, there are Russian ethnics fleeing or living in fear in all of the far reaches of the former Soviet Union. Add this to the fact that political boundaries rarely conform to national or ethnic ones and it seems clear that unless strong preventive measures are taken, there will be nationalist and ethnic trouble in the former Soviet Union for a long time.

It would take a complete volume to review the ethnic disturbances that have occurred in the former Soviet republics since 1990. There has been rioting between Kirghiz and Uzbeks in Kirghizia and between Uzbeks and Meskhetial Turks in Uzbekistan. There has also been ethnic violence in central Asia in Turkmenistan and Tajikistan. In Azerbaijan there is no peace between warring Azeris and Armenian ethnics. Only three of the five million people living in Georgia are Georgians and there has been constant ethnic conflict before and after Georgia's declaration of independence. By September 1993 that new nation was in a state of armed rebellion.

The war for independence in Chechnia continued into the new millennium. By then, Russia had exhibited a wide range of responses to former Soviet states. Like the Americans in Vietnam, the Russians destroyed Chechnia in order to save it. In Georgia they chose a policy of harassment, which Baker describes as intimidation and blackmail.[47] As for the Baltic states, the Russians simply turned their backs and walked away.

Barber tells us that in 1991 there were more than thirty wars in progress, "most of them ethnic, racial, tribal, or religious in character."[48] Nation-states have had to deal with problems of minority peoples everywhere in the world and from time immemorial. Dissolution of oppressive totalitarian regimes into more democratic ones results in a new rash of national and ethnic problems. Maier, writing on Nigeria, sums it up this way:

> Indeed the spread of virulent strains of chauvinism in Nigeria is part of a world-wide phenomenon playing out in Indonesia, the Balkans, the former Soviet Union, and a host of other African nations. This sort of politicized tribalism, a constant companion to the modern version of globalization, is the biggest threat to international peace and stability. With ever growing frequency wars are fought not between states but within them. The conflict is neighbor against neighbor, us against them, always the menacing Other, whether the differences are racial, religious, or linguistic.[49]

What solutions have the nations of the world discovered for such problems? What kinds of policies have been attempted? What kinds are emerging in the contemporary world and what in all of this appears useful for peoples attempting to enjoy democratic self-government? These questions stand at the heart of this volume. But there is another one which precedes them. What is the source of this intergroup antipathy? What are its origins? In truth, the answer to that question is complex and multifaceted, but I will venture for the reader's consideration a possible historical explanation in chapter 3.

Notes

1. Benjamin R. Barber, "Jihad vs. McWorld," *The Atlantic* 269, no. 3 (March 1992): 53-63.

2. Douglas Farah, "Nigerians Await Democracy's Dividends," *Washington Post*, 27 April 2000, 21–22(A).

3. Jennifer Parmelee, "Ethiopia Plies Democracy Contentiously," *Washington Post*, 22 October 1991, 18(A).

4. Richard Rose, William Mischler, and Christian Herpfer, *Democracy and Its Alternatives: Understanding Post-Communist Societies* (Baltimore, Md.: Johns Hopkins University Press, 1998).

5. James Rupert, "Central Asia Faces Struggle over Future," *Washington Post*, 19 December 1991, 41(A).

6. Jim Hoagland, "Human Rights and Our Allies," *Washington Post*, 10 March 2002, 9(B).

7. From a London Press conference reported in the *Dayton* [Ohio] *Daily News*, 29

January 1992.

8. Conor Cruise O'Brien, "Nationalists and Democrats," *New York Times Review of Books*, 15 August 1991, 29–31.

9. Vladimir Meciar, "Slovenia Is a Model for Slovakia," *The Economist*, 13 September 1991, 54.

10. Jim Hoagland, "Model Systems—Warts and All," *Washington Post*, 30 March 2000, 21(A).

11. Alexis de Toccqueville, *Democracy in America*, trans. Henry Reeve, 2 vols. (New York: The Colonial Press, 1899), chapters 15 and 16.

12. For a metaphoric treatment of this period see Gary Alan Fine and Lazaros Christoforides , "Dirty Birds, Filthy Immigrants, and the English Sparrow War: Metaphorical Linkage in Constructing Social Problems" (paper presented at the annual meeting of the Society for the Study of Social Problems, Cincinnati, Ohio, August 1991).

13. Peter Baker, "Va. Family Victims of Cruel Error," *Washington Post*, 19 February 1991, 1 and 3(B).

14. Alan Cooperman, "Sept. 11 Backlash Murders and the State of 'Hate,'" *Washington Post*, 20 January 2002, 3 and 14(A). For a scholarly collection of papers dealing with hate crimes see Jack Levin and Gordana Rabrenovic, eds., *Hate Crimes and Ethnic Conflict: A Comparative Perspective* (Thousand Oaks, Calif.: Sage Publications, 2001).

15. Michael Massing, *Washington Post*, 23 December 1990, 18(A).

16. Donald T. Campbell, "Conversations" public discussion at the annual meeting of the Evaluation Research Society, Arlington, Va. (1980).

17. Edward Walsh, "Letters from the County Clerk's Office," *Washington Post*, 19 September 1991, 3(A).

18. Fred Hiatt, "Soviet Backlash Mounts against Democratization," *Washington Post*, 12 November 1991, 18(A).

19. Sharon LaFraniere, "In Latvia Officials Wage War of Words," *Washington Post*, 11 March 2001, 18(A).

20. Kenneth J. Varum, "Crime Statistics," *New Outlook: A Quarterly Publication of the American Committee on U.S.-Soviet Relations* 11, no. 2 (spring 1991): 74-75. See also the Associated Press dateline 29 July 1992, "Russian Crime Rise Laid to Economic Ills," *Washington Post*, 29 July 1992, 17(A).

21. Population Crisis Committee, *Cities: Life in the World's 100 Largest Metropolitan Areas* (Washington, D.C., 1991).

22. Kara Swisher, "With Unity There Also Is Worry," *Washington Post*, 9 September 1992, 1(F), 4 (F).

23. Blaine Harden, "Walesa Promises to Continue Free Market Despite Vote," *Washington Post*, 28 October 1992.

24. Marlisa Simons, "Uneasy Czechoslovaks Ending Free Health Care," *New York Times*, 17 December 1992, 3 (A).

25. Margaret Shapiro, "Hunger and Hardship from the Baltic to the Caucasus," *Washington Post*, 28 January 1992.

26. Mary Battiata, "East Europe Hunts for Ex-Reds," *Washington Post*, 28 December 1991.

27. Quoted by Mary Battiata, "Pope Begins Visit to Different Poland," *Washington Post*, 2 June 1991, 21(A), 27(A).

28. For an introduction to Weber's work in English see Hans H. Gerth and C. Wright Mills, trans. and eds., *From Max Weber: Essays in Sociology* (New York: Oxford Univer-

sity Press, 1946). In a personal communication, the German sociologist Horst Jurgen Helle informed me after reading the paper on which this chapter is based that the term "Iron Cage" is an artifact of Talcott Parsons' translation. "Weber," according to Helle, "writes about 'das stahlharte Gehaeuse' which would more precisely be translated as a lodging as hard as steel." Helle states that Weber's metaphor is intended to conjure up an image of a loss of flexibility rather than of imprisonment.

29. Gerth and Mills, *From Max Weber*.

30. See Fred Hiatt, "Lithuania's Step Backward," *Washington Post*, 23 December 1992, 1(A) and 20(A); Paul Lenvai, "A New Crop of Dictators," *Washington Post*, 5 February 1993, 25(A).

31. Jack Anderson and Dale Van Atta, *Washington Post*, 15 December 1991.

32. Mary Erdmans, "Why Poles Stay: The Morality of Hanging in There" (paper presented at the annual meeting of the Society for Applied Sociology, Cincinnati, Ohio, October 1990).

33. Dita Smith, "They've Come a Long Way, But. . . . ." (Citing data provided by the Interparliamentary Union, Worldwatch Institute) in *Washington Post*, 10 June 2000, 16(A).

34. Katalin Kovacs, "The Consequences for Women of the Changing Hungarian Political Economy (paper presented at the annual meeting of the American Sociological Association, Cincinnati, Ohio, August 1991).

35. Reported by Richard Morin, "Europe's Dark Expectations," *Washington Post*, 19 May 1991, 2(D).

36. Reported by Michael Z. Wise, "Polls Show Anti-semitism Persisting in Austria," *Washington Post*, 24 October 1991.

37. Poll published in *Evenement de Jeudi* and cited in *Dateline: World Jewry* (New York: World Jewish Congress, October, 1991).

38. Poll published in *Evenement*, 1991. Horst Jurgen Helle, in a second bit of advice, reminds me that the rates of prejudice may be equal in both parts of Germany. He attributes the apparent lower percentage in eastern Germany to decades of conditioning to say only what was expected and to a well-developed intuition about what the other person would like to hear. He believes that the tradition of independence in western Germany is more likely to result in people giving their opinions freely regardless of what they think others may expect. Helle's explanation reconciles the apparent contradiction found in my statement on page 19 that this sort of bigotry had migrated from the east to the west.

39. Douglas Farah, "Nigerians Await Democracy's Dividends," *Washington Post*, 27 April 2000, 21–22(A).

40. Steve Coll, "Flood of Minority Muslims Flees Repression by Myanmar's Junta," *Washington Post*, 6 February, 1992.

41. Molly Moore, "Tajiks Trade One Nightmare for Another," *Washington Post*, 19, January 1993.

42. Dan Pavel, "Romania's Hidden Victims: Wanderers," *New Republic* (March 4, 1991): 12-13.

43. Annelise Orleck, *The Soviet Jewish Americans* (Westport, Conn.: Greenwood Press, 1999).

44. Mary Battiata, *Washington Post*, 30 September 1991.

45. Gary Lee, *Washington Post*, 30 September 1991.

46. Michael Dobbs, "The Empire of Ethnic Russians Retrenches," *Washington Post*, 7 October 1990, 1(A) and 34-35(A). A year later, Dobbs finds that things have not changed: "Ethnic Strife Splintering Core of Russian Republic," *Washington Post*, 29 October 1991,

1(A) and 19(A).

47. Peter Baker, "For Georgia, Russia Remains an Intimidating Neighbor," *Washington Post*, 6 May 2001, 23(A).

48. Benjamin R. Barber, "Jihad vs. McWorld," *The Atlantic* (March 1992): 53-63.

49. Karl Maier, *This House Has Fallen: Midnight in Nigeria* (New York: Public Affairs, 2000), xx.

Chapter 3

The Invention of Race and Ethnicity and Its Many Consequences

In an age of nationalist and imperialist expansion national pride played no small part in the naming and classification of fossil as well as of living forms of men. If the concept of race had not existed it would have had to be invented during this period.... The concept of race ... should be dropped from the vocabulary of the anthropologist, for it has done an infinite amount of harm and no good at all.

—Ashley Montagu, ed., *The Concept of Race* (Glencoe, Ill.: Free Press, 1964)

Perhaps it was not quite as exotic as Calcutta or Prague, but a symposium celebrating the Columbian Quincentenary in Baton Rouge, Louisiana, was equally stimulating. The Mississippi levies were a lot bigger than the dikes separating the rice fields in West Bengal, and there were no threatening watch towers along that muddy river as there had been along the Danube. With Huey Long's tower of the Louisiana state capitol building looming over us, a group of scholars, mostly authorities on Hispanic language and literatures, considered the legacy of Christopher Columbus. My contribution concerned the notions of race and ethnicity as they evolved following Columbus's "discovery" of the new world. It was February 1992 and what follows are my comments bolstered by some of the things I learned from others at that symposium.

The Colonial Heritage

It was suggested more than once that Columbus cannot be credited with discovering America, since it was already there. I thought that may be true and it certainly seemed that the Americans at that time appeared to have no interest in discovering Europe. Regardless of the merits of that argument, there is an authentic discovery—or, more precisely, an "invention"—which resulted in part from Columbus's voyages. It is the discovery of something which did not exist before. That invention, which evolved from the sixteenth century through the nineteenth and persists to this day, is the notion of race. The earliest reference I have seen to the relationship between skin color and "superiority" appears in the seventh century. Hooper observes that the prophet Muhammad said in his last sermon, "A white person has no superiority over a black person, nor a black has any superiority over white except by piety and good action."[1] This spiritual prescription anticipates Ashley Montagu's scientific one by nearly 1,400 years. It implies that racial prejudices may be considerably more ancient than I am assuming in this chapter. Nevertheless, In his analysis of the "tall tale of discovery" (both Columbian and scientific) ilter reminds us that it is "no accident that the history of 'discovery' is *also* the history of colonialism and imperialism."[2]

It is also true that the fiesta, "*El dia de la raza*" (called Columbus Day in the United States), might better have been called "The day of race relations" rather than of "the race," for it celebrates the day on which they may be said to have commenced.[3] The invention of race, as useful as it may have been for emerging colonial powers, left a troublesome legacy to the twentieth century world. At a meeting In December 1991 of politicians, bureaucrats, and activists from European cities, a member of the European Parliament reminded the gathering that, "Racism is scientifically nonsensical, morally wrong but, most of all, politically dangerous."[4] Some thirty years earlier a distinguished anthropologist announced to his colleagues that "Races are products of the past. They are relics of times and conditions which have long ceased to exist."[5]

The concept of race had been useful in justifying slavery and other forms of oppression of indigenous peoples. Describing the origins of physical anthropology in mid-nineteenth-century America, Hogben finds that, "Reference to the literature of the time abundantly discloses . . . the hope of demonstrating that the African Negro is more primitive in a zoological sense than the Southern Gentry and their supporters."[6] The persistence of these and related notions, both in Europe and America, is evidenced by the attendance of leaders from cities throughout Europe at the Birmingham meeting of December 1991. It was there that Glyn Ford reminded Europe that, among other things, racism is scientifically nonsensical. Although I am in accord with Mr. Ford's sentiments, my focus is, nevertheless, on the scientific dimension. Why do I focus on an admittedly "nonsensical" dimension? Surely the concept is no longer employed by zoologists, biologists, physical anthropologists or geneticists. But for the cultural anthropologist, the sociologist, the social psychologist, and the political scientist, a monster has been created.[7]

At an international conference on race and ethnicity, Marshall Segall offered an impressive presentation on the Human Genome Project. It was the spring of 2001 in Oxford, Mississippi—a place of some historic note in American race relations. He informed us that "we all share 99.9 percent of our genes with everyone else in the human race." He announced that "it is an indisputable fact that post-DNA research in genetics, coupled with recent studies in paleontology and anthropology, have made 'race' an invalid concept."[8] When I suggested to him that social scientists had long known that the concept of race was no more than a social construct, he responded solemnly: "That is true but now we have *real* scientific evidence and that will be more convincing to people." Perhaps, but I doubt that the monster can be put to rest that easily.

Race survives as a reality in the minds of contemporary peoples all over the world. Since ordinary people believe that race is real, they act toward others as if it were real, and those actions have visibly real consequences for both dominant and minority peoples worldwide. This notion of social reality is not original with me. W. I. Thomas suggested it in 1923.[9] Nor is the thesis that the source of contemporary racial and ethnic conflicts lies in the policies and practices of colonial powers. I have mentioned the rich contributions of the participants in the Louisiana State University conference, and they were not alone. Kinloch, for example, devotes a whole book to the demonstration of a high positive correlation between the degree of colonial influence and the degree of intergroup hostilities.[10]

I do not intend to argue that the European imperial powers were the first to conquer and mistreat alien peoples. Shils reminds us that long before Columbus set out on his portentous expedition, "Asians had conquered other Asians; Arabs had exploited and enslaved black Africans, often with the aid of other black African rulers. Still it is the European conquest that is remembered."[11] Shils believes it differs from its predecessors because of its more recent occurrence and visible consequences as well as the hypocrisy of a religion and a politics which it failed to adhere to at home and all but ignored in its conquered domains. Furthermore, rather than being expanding neighbors, the European conquerors came from far off and they were of a different color.

These are important differences especially when considered within their historic milieu. Under Queen Isabella, the Spanish Inquisition began in 1478. It was aimed first at punishing Jews. It was extended to include Moslems, and eventually (as such things go) to anyone suspected of heresy. According to Tullia Zevi Isabella's reign destroyed "a unique example of fruitful cooperation among Jews, Moslems and Christians."[12] In 1492 Isabella's troops finally defeated the Moors and drove them from Spain along with the Jews who had flourished there for nearly fifteen centuries. In today's world, this dirty process is referred to as "ethnic cleansing" by Serbs who invented it and shortly after by Croats who appeared to approve of the idea. Early in the 1990s the descriptive term was widely understood in the English-speaking world. The siege of Sarajevo in 1992 is little different from the siege of Cordoba in 1492. Such was the religious and political climate at the time Columbus set sail. There is no reason to believe that he entertained ideologies which varied from those of his benevolent sponsor and those pervading the European world he left behind.

It would be less than fair to ignore the Protestant colonizers, whose theology, although it took a different route, ended at the same destination so far as native peoples were concerned:

> When the Calvinists came to America and found themselves in the presence of pagan Indians, it was perfectly natural that they should set about with missionary fervor to destroy the corrupt nature of these pagans. . . . The Indian had only to give up his natural liberty, which was anarchical, troublesome and diabolical, and bow to the superior law of the Christians as laid down in the Good Book. Unfortunately the Indian preferred his liberty to servitude and his diabolical practices to the rules of Holy Writ.[13]

Leaping ahead in history, we find this Calvinist theology surviving into the dawn of the twenty first century. Bastide argues that in South Africa the Calvinist attitude was institutionalized in the form of apartheid. "White culture," he writes, "becomes identified with defense of the faith." It also survives in more subtle forms as in Great Britain where those nomadic peoples known as "wanderers" or "travelers" persist in their stubborn refusal to "adjust" to British and Irish society. Although the Calvinist worldview may explain British antipathy toward the "wanderers," it fails to explain the Irish hostility they face.

Lavery reminds us that the wanderers are of Celtic origin, largely Roman Catholic, poor, and otherwise culturally similar to most other Irish people. He is puzzled by the fact that Ireland's newfound desire to be tolerant and diverse does not extend to these travelers.[14] It may well be their lifestyle which brings such contempt down upon them—perhaps similar to the suspicion and hostility many Americans felt in the 1960s toward their "long haired hippie freak" fellow Americans. Joyce makes the clear distinction between a pathological group which is in need of rehabilitation so that it can return to the larger society from which it has strayed and, on the other hand, an ethnic group which is in important ways "different" and values its differences.[15]

The colonists appear to have viewed all indigenous peoples as pathological—in need of rehabilitation (i.e., Christianizing). Had the colonists, both Catholic and Protestant, been able to grasp their own ethnocentrism—to view native peoples as ethnically unlike themselves, then we would suffer only the consequences of their greed and the history of the world might be somewhat different. Perhaps those Native American groups from many places in the Western Hemisphere who issued a set of resolutions in Kuna Yala, Panama, would not have commemorated the quincentennial as "The Five Hundredth Anniversary of the European Invasion."[16]

Returning through time to the end of the sixteenth century, which had begun with Columbus's voyages, we find William Shakespeare[17] creating amusing tales for the consumption of ordinary English folk. In *Othello*, subtitled "The Moor of Venice," he makes much of color, if not of race. The pervasiveness of an anti-

Semitism, rooted in the Christianity of the day, provides the basis for the Bard's *Merchant of Venice*. By now, color and religion were commonly understood discriminators among peoples. Commentators such as Pitt-Rivers[18] (and myself) are sometimes guilty of assuming causation when the evidence is largely correlational. We attribute race and ethnicity to the Age of Discovery because the two happened together. Hirschman is more generous in his explanation:

> Then about 1500 or so, the development of regular long distance transportation led to an integrated world system and considerable population movements throughout the world. A related change over the last 100 to 200 years has been the formation of states with boundaries that span the "traditional" geographical homes of different ethnic groups. The result of these changes has been the creation of multiethnic societies in every part of the globe.[19]

This is a description of the beginnings of what is now commonly called "globalization." My chapter title speaks of ethnicity as well as race. Cushing observes sarcastically that "self-conscious ethnic group identification is an emergent phenomenon, a residue from [the] colonial experience and other joys of European contact."[20] It does appear that "ethnicity," like "race," is a colonial invention which continues to flourish. In the 1920s the Soviets attempted to dissolve a pan-Turkic nationalism in central Asia by dividing the region into republics, each with an assigned language, alphabet, and national identity: "People were encouraged to think of themselves as Turkmens, Uzbeks, Kazakhs, or Kirghiz—distinctions that previously had carried little significance."[21]

A parallel is provided by middle-class residents of Sarajevo who had thought of themselves as Bosnians. They complained of the sudden imposition of a Muslim, Serbian, Croatian, or Jewish identity.[22] In 1992, prior to the ascendency of the Taliban (and its destruction by American bombers) the president of Afghanistan's new interim ruling council bemoaned the creation of ethnicity in that country: "Nowadays, people say of someone that He 'is a Tajik' or 'He is a Pashtun,'" Mojadidi said. "You should not think about this. We should make a just integration."[23]

Even though "ethnicity" may be a colonial invention, the concept allows an alternative to a dominant group's definition of other people as pathological. Studies of both Pacific Island peoples and those of Africa conclude that the concept of ethnicity is alien to many colonial peoples. They do, however, find it useful in dealing with their colonial overlords. According to Gauthier and Fawcett, "The [New Zealand] Maori fought to maintain their identity in the face of the ethnocentric colonizers by modifying their culture to fight more effectively."[24] That modification consisted of adopting the devices of the colonial rulers as weapons to be used against them: "First they created institutions similar to those of the British, the idea being to create systems that would be recognized but also conflict with the enforced ones."

Linnekin and Poyer argue that among Pacific Islanders, ethnicity is a

Western-imposed concept. These peoples traditionally stratified themselves along what the writers call a Lamarckian model in which external characteristics such as environment, behavior, or situation are more important in defining a person's position in society than are biological and ancestral heritage. Because such characteristics are subject to radical change, they contrast sharply with the Western notion of ethnicity.[25] Linnekin and Poyer describe ethnicity as a Mendelian model where group identification is involuntary, has clear boundaries, and is determined by genetic origins. It is nevertheless troublesome that the colonial ideology seemed to pervade the native Fijian objection to elected leaders of Indian heritage when a coup overthrew the latter in the spring of 2000.

The ten ethnographies in the Linnekin and Poyer volume, each of a different Pacific people, clearly support their central contention that it is the Western idea of ethnicity which becomes integral to colonial law, education, and other social institutions. Pacific islanders respond by developing their own ethnic identities as a device to resist the colonials within their own framework. Parallel evidence is reported from Africa, where Newbury describes the development of ethnic identity in Rwanda under German and Belgian administrations, "as a marker of political immunity or vulnerability." According to Newbury there is nothing primordial about ethnicity in Africa.[26]

In a paper aimed at distinguishing between race and ethnicity, and based on the premise that races are the product of Western colonialism, Blauner differs sharply with Linnekin and Poyers genetic definition of ethnicity, For Blauner an ethnic group is simply one "that shares a common past or believes it does. Ethnic groups hold a set of common memories which make members of that group feel distinctive in their customs, culture, and outlook."[27] It is not necessary to enter into a debate over definitions. It is sufficient to say that both race and ethnicity are ideas imposed upon indigenous peoples for the benefit of the conquerors. They are devices which enable the predator to cage the prey. As the evidence indicates, minorities may also find ethnicity to be something they can make use of. Beyond that, this imposed identity can, as Blauner suggests, contribute to a sense of peoplehood and an awareness of a common fate. It can be turned into an instrument of solidarity and collective pride among the very peoples it was designed to denigrate.

In the early 1990s the rash of contemporary literature on the Quincentenary tended to be polarized. On the one hand we find the angry reminders by native peoples and their supporters of the terrible deeds done by Columbus and those who followed. On the other hand, and equally volatile, were the American conservatives with their deep suspicion of multiculturalism, multilingualism, revisionist history, and all things alien to what they see as the true American heritage. Achenbach, for example, writing of what he terms the anti-Columbian reaction argues: "The rejection of modern America requires a kind of intellectual surgery in which society is carefully tweezed apart into incompatible and confrontational elements. The idea of the 'melting pot,'" he claims, "is considered reactionary: it robs people of their ethnic heritage." He suggests that the idea of difference can become fetishistic and reminds us of certain similarities between peoples of the old and new worlds: "Columbus left 39 sailors on the island of Hispaniola after the Santa Maria was shipwrecked. All 39 were killed by natives (probably with good reason, say many historians)."[28]

Having created these new distinctions among peoples, how then did the dominant nations of the world deal with them? As we turn from ancient history to contemporary politics (and sometimes scholarship), let us consider the consequences of the discovery of race and ethnicity and the subsequent violence it has done to the physical and cultural worlds on which it was imposed. Since race and ethnicity are now deeply imbedded in popular consciousness and since they are the source of much international and intranational conflict, the question of policy arises. How can peoples resolve these issues?

Solving the Problem: One Way or Another

The dominant group (which need not be a numerical majority) can impose its will on the minority group (which need not be a numerical minority) in different ways. These depend upon the extent to which the minority is viewed as useful to the dominant and the extent of power the dominant possesses to impose its will upon the minority. Historically, efforts to solve perceived minority problems have included *assimilation* as in the case of Ceausescu's Romania, *pluralism* as in the case of Canada's fragile multicultural policy, and *territorial segregation* as in Switzerland, apartheid South Africa, tribal India, or contemporary Belgium.

Scapegoating is another useful policy and is flexible enough to be used in conjunction with any of the others. It has proved politically useful to those in power in many parts of the world. Convenient scapegoats in recent history include migratory east Indians, Jews, Chinese, and Gypsies (Roma) almost anywhere they are found. It has been suggested that in contemporary Romania it is government policy to encourage anti-Gypsy feelings. Many Romanians "believe the Gypsies not only are responsible for everybody else's troubles, but are prospering on account of them."[29] *Annihilation* of the minority is a solution employed by Spain and the United States in their early dealings with native American populations. For a time it was the policy of the French Revolution in disposing of the aristocracy and other "enemies of the people." More recently this policy was employed by Nazi Germany toward both Gypsies and Jews, by the Stalinist Soviet Union toward the Polish educated classes, and, it is sometimes argued, by Turkey toward Armenians.

In Rwanda we find an up-to-date 1990s version of this policy of deliberately destroying a people. It is, however, rare that an effort is made to completely eliminate a people. The Nazis may have provided the defining case but surely the Hutu government of Rwanda came closest to succeeding. Power describes it as "the fastest most efficient killing spree of the twentieth century."[30] She also reminds us that genocide is defined not by how many people are killed, but by the intent of the killers. Thus, although it is in fact not genocide, an effort to remove a people from a locality by force and fear can result in considerably more suffering, masses of refugees, as well as the destruction of homes and villages. In the late twentieth century Serbs, Croats, and sometimes Israelis were simply intent on ridding their territory of unsavory others. Whether those others lived or died was not relevant.

Expulsion, whether voluntary or forced, is another possibility as witnessed by the mass migrations of both Muslems and Hindus at the time of the partition of India and Pakistan or the departure of ethnic Turks from Bulgaria or the mass flight of Kurds from Iraq in the 1990s. In the nineteenth century when gold was discovered in the southern Appalachians, Americans drove the entire Cherokee Indian tribe (among others) from their southern cotton plantations. They were forced west on a death march along what became known as the trail of tears. These Native Americans lost not only their homes and their land but their slaves too.

What is referred to by Serbs and Croats in Bosnia as "ethnic cleansing" is essentially a contemporary version of the expulsion processes blended with annihilation of the "others" when they are unable or unwilling to exit quickly enough. The final instance of such a policy occurred at the end of the millennium when Serbs expelled the Kosovar population from Kosovo. With the intervention of the international community, the process was reversed as the Serb population fled in panic when the Kosovars returned.

A laissez-faire policy, although infrequent, can be found as in the case of turn of the twentieth century European immigrants to the United States who gravitated toward assimilation as a consequence both of the exclusively English institutions (educational, political, social welfare, health, etc.) provided for them and the pressure of new waves of immigrants following them from other parts of Europe. Perhaps the relations between Jews and Muslims in Moorish Spain was such a case, although it is, by and large, difficult to imagine a dominant group simply leaving a minority alone.

A possibility which is imposed when the minority is needed to provide a cheap labor force is *slavery or some form of serfdom* as employed by Hungarian landlords in Slovakia prior to World War I or by the British in Ireland well into the twentieth century. According to the London-based Anti-Slavery Society, slavery is widespread in the contemporary world. Chattel slavery (the total ownership of one person by another) was not outlawed on the Arabian Peninsula until the early 1970s and may be expanding in parts of northern Africa, particularly Sudan. Far more prevalent is debt bondage in which in effect one rents a slave rather than owning one. It is a form of forced labor found among Haitians living illegally in the Dominican Republic. In parts of Asia such slavery has become a routinized form of child abuse whether as labor in Indian rug factories or prostitution in Thailand.[31]

There is also a phenomenon which Georg Simmel identified late in the nineteenth century as the *tertius gaudens*—the third party who gains. The notion of "irredentism" must benefit a bordering minority which is reclaimed from one nation by another when the latter extends its border to be more inclusive. In this century German claims on German-speaking territories in France, Austria, and Czechoslovakia provide examples. Irredentism threatens many of the states bordering western Russia and with the breakup of Czechoslovakia, the Hungarian majority in the east of the new Slovakia may well seek protection from Hungary and possibly surviving Germans in the Czech Sudentenland will once again look wistfully to their motherland.

Both the Soviets and the Americans adopted a policy of *tertius gaudens* in their pursuit of the cold war. With the end of that conflict, African client states were quickly abandoned by both parties. The support of tribal hill people by the United States in Afganistan in the 1980s for no better reason than to annoy the Soviets illustrates this type of *tertius gaudens*. From time to time the Kurdish people have enjoyed the support of Iran—when it was at war with Iraq—and of the United States when they irritated the Soviets. But when the United States needed Turkey's support in its quarrel with Iraq, the Kurds found themselves out in the cold for a very long time. The tide appeared to turn again in favor of the Kurds when world opinion forced the American president to reverse his "non-interference-in internal-affairs" policy and come to the aid of Kurdish refugees following the Iraqi cease-fire in 1991. Such is the fate of the *tertius gaudens*.

A final policy sometimes emerges when economic shifts render slavery or forced labor no longer useful to the dominant group. What can then result is a policy of *dumping and containing* such "used-up" minorities. Such people are set aside with restricted access to resources and to movement. This was the experience of both post-slavery blacks in the United States and post-World War II Koreans in Japan. Perhaps a subcategory of this essentially territorial solution is the *Zoo Solution*, in which quaint remainders of peoples such as Laplanders (Sami) in Sweden or some smaller tribes of Native Americans or indigenous Australians become national curios exhibited in their "natural habitat" for the amusement and entertainment of the dominant group.

There are surely other possibilities. Human imagination seems boundless when it comes to creating punishing policies toward minority people. How does one classify British policy in Northern Ireland until the year 2000, or the forced importation of alien peoples as slave labor as in the case of Africans shipped to the United States, Brazil, and other places in South America, or Koreans forced to migrate to Japan during World War II? A different variant occurs when the minority (usually because it sees its culture as superior) chooses to isolate itself from the dominant group. Both the Roma and ultra-orthodox Jews are contemptuous of host societies while the Amish find it agreeable and profitable to accept a definition of themselves as "cute."

To complicate matters, it seems that no policy is permanent. Perhaps due to the volatility of group sentiments as well as the fortunes of war and politics, policy can shift over time and usually does. In the twenty-first century, a backlash against pluralism is developing in Canada. An extreme example of this is the passing of legislation in one city calling for the removal of all bilingual signs and mandating English as the only official language (Ironically, the name of that city is *Sault St. Marie*). The Romanians have abandoned their forced assimilation of Hungarians. Americans, Germans, and Turks no longer maintain a policy of annihilation toward certain minorities within their own borders. It is entirely possible that there are cycles through which national policies may move. For example, annihilation may be pursued only so long as the minority remains large enough to be perceived as threatening. Once the minority is reduced to manageable proportions, it becomes easier and cheaper to relegate it to a zoo. This would not satisfy the Nazis or the Serbs but Americans and Australians seemed to find it a practical policy shift.

The Exclusion of Immoral Solutions

In spite of the difficulties imposed by the volatility of these policies and in spite of the capacity of policymakers to apply simultaneously combinations of them, we have at least a hint at the many possible solutions to ethnic "problems." I have made an effort to identify the range of historic national policies toward minorities. Some of these, as politically and economically expedient as they might be, are indeed very dark on purely moral grounds. In later chapters I will exclude from my consideration of solutions slavery or any form of forced labor, expulsion, annihilation, or physically removing and caging minorities on reservations. I do not know of anyone who argues that it benefits minorities to be killed, enslaved, or exported. There are, however, those who argue that it benefits indigenous minorities economically and physically as well as preserves their culture, when the dominant group isolates them in zoos. Here their music, art, and colorful costumes can be admired, health care provided, and handicrafts sold. I disagree and will explain my position below.

For the moment it should be clear that certain policies have been eliminated from consideration on moral grounds. Perhaps this is the place to point out that the atrocities committed against minorities have been historically and continue to be for the most part religiously motivated or at least religiously justified. As we shall see the most peaceful of religious ideologies, Buddhism and Hinduism, have fallen prey to the model of religious intolerance provided by their more numerous Christian and Muslim brethren. It is particularly tragic to observe the squalor and oppression suffered by Palestinian citizens in the Jewish state of Israel. It may be that Sir Arthur C. Clarke is correct when he asserts: "One of the greatest tragedies in human history was the hijacking of morality by religion." The main purpose of this book is to identify solutions to intergroup conflict that work without hurting people. Solutions that inflict pain and suffering have been eliminated from consideration no matter how effective they might be.

Before moving on, let us mull over the puzzling pros and cons of the zoo solution. The title, coined by Woon,[32] is itself prejudicial and thus unfair. It is an alternative which suggests that a minority, in this case indigenous peoples, can be protected by isolating them from the dominant group in certain areas reserved exclusively for them. It has either been pursued or proposed in the United States, Canada, Brazil, Australia, northern Scandinavia, and perhaps elsewhere. Recall that dumping and containing is most likely to occur when slavery or forced labor loses its economic viability. These "used up minorities" are then relegated to ghettos, reservations, or homelands. They are isolated physically from the dominant group, identified as second-class people, and then denied access to housing, work, education, other societal rights and privileges and to the same civil rights enjoyed by the dominant group. This was the fate of most former slaves in the Americas and is the fate today of the descendants of Korean laborers forcibly imported to Japan during World War II.[33] A Norwegian anthropologist argues that there are two role choices open to such minorities: they may, she says, be either "mute" or "cute."[34] The isolation of dumping and containing is one way to keep a minority mute, but what does Woon intend by "cute"? We will come to that in a moment.

There is a final policy that sometimes emerges in this line from forced labor to dumping and containing. It is the protected reserve—the policy of isolating the minority for its own protection and preservation. Sometimes the intention is a benign effort to save a disappearing culture or a dwindling people. For those who view assimilation as undesirable, this " zoo" solution provides an alternative. Peruvian policy illustrates how the zoo can be viewed as a possibly desirable alternative to assimilation. It is of course true that sometimes the intentions of assimilationist policies are far from benign. We will take a closer look at the pros and cons of assimilationist policies in chapter 13. For the moment let us consider Peru.

Peruvian policy provides an instance which highlights the controversial nature of even benign efforts to promote the assimilation of indigenous peoples. It raises the question: from whose perspective is the darkness of a policy defined? Robinson observes that millions of Peruvians have migrated from the countryside to Lima in recent years and "almost immediately they abandon the traditional rural costumes. Long skirts and pigtails give way to stone-washed blue jeans, Michael Jackson T-shirts and curly permanents. Self-image also changes: Indians become mestizos."[35] (Mestizos are persons of mixed Indian and European ancestry.) He insists that 'The Peruvian state encourages this process of transfor- mation." As with all minority policies there are strong feelings about this one. Robinson interviewed Diego Garcia-Sayan, head of the Andean Commission of Jurists, a human rights organization. According to Garcia-Sayan, "When the

Indian comes to the city and dresses like a mestizo, speaks Spanish instead of Quechua, goes to school and all that, he ceases being an Indian, the Indian is forced to whiten himself." Garcia-Sayan describes this process as discrimination although it appears to be one that both native Peruvians and their government prefer.

When an indigenous minority is close to annihilation and is reduced to dependence upon the dominant group, it may be that the only alternative is a policy of "artificial isolation as a kind of theme park exhibit" as Robinson describes Brazilian policy toward its natives in the upper Amazon region in a follow-up article (June 24). In 1991 the Brazilian government made an effort to preserve and protect the remaining native peoples of the upper Amazon. They expelled the 20,000 miners who had invaded the area in search of gold. A study commission was appointed to decide whether to make the area a permanent preserve. Robinson is not alone in his concern. This is precisely what our Norwegian anthropologist has described as a "cute" minority. Woon claims that this happens when a government decides to protect those among the remaining fragments of a former peoples who wish to preserve their traditional culture. Usually this involves a protected area, heavily subsidized by the dominant group, sometimes economically viable as a result of a tourist economy. Cases of this type include some native Americans, the Ainu of northern Japan, possibly the Laplanders (Sami) of northern Scandinavia (about whom Woon was speaking) and perhaps the Australian aborigines. Woon's references to putting people in a zoo is what Robinson intended by his theme park metaphor.

Brazil sits smack up against Peru. On November 15, 1991, Brazil's president Fernando Collor de Mello issued a decree granting "permanent rights over 36,358 square miles of dense Amazon rain forest to [the Yanomami Indians] whose population has dwindled to 10,000."[36] In January 1992, under orders from a Brazilian federal judge, authorities were notified to immediately remove all gold miners from Nambiquara lands. These people, totaling about 800 individuals, live in western Brazil.[37] This type of policy may be less than desirable, but with both the Peruvian Mestizos and the Brazilian Indians, existing policies appear to reflect the will of the minority group. The one appears to prefer European ways while the other would preserve its indigenous language and traditions. Self-determination is a reasonable criterion of the morality of such policies. They can hardly be seen as "dark" under such conditions. The Brazilian solution closely resembles that negotiated by Canada's Inuit Eskimo people with the Canadian government.[38] Here too we find vast amounts of sparsely populated land (In this case Arctic tundra rather than tropical rainforest) allocated to a small population (17,000).

Clearly, there is no place among civilized nations for such painful minority policies as extermination, slavery, expulsion, or dumping and containing. One would prefer that no society would permit matters to evolve to the point where the only choice for survival of the minority culture lies in a theme park policy.

They then become a living museum protected by the state and prospering from the tourists. In this chapter we have taken note of human inventiveness in discovering the ideas of race and ethnicity and our further creativity in manufacturing social devices to accommodate that invention. All of this has been viewed largely from the perspective of the inventors. In chapter 4 we will shift to the meaning ethnicity has to the inventees. We will look at what ethnicity means to contemporary people—mostly American people—in the last quarter of the last century. How do they define themselves in this context?

Notes

1. Ibrahim Hooper, "Slavery and Stereotypes," *Washington Post*, 17 January 1998, 23(A).

2. Tugrul ilter, "The White Mythology of Discovery: From Discovering the 'New World' through Discovering 'Facts' to George Bush's "New World" Order(s)." (paper read at a symposium *Rediscovering American 1492-1992*. Louisiana State University, Baton Rouge, Louisiana, 27 February 1992).

3. Julian Pitt-Rivers, "Race, Color, and Class in Central America and the Andes," *Daedalus* (spring 1967): 542-59.

4. Glyn Ford, "Race Relations in the European Community" (Address presented at the International Conference on Racial Equality in Europe. Birmingham, England, 3 December 1991).

5. S. L. Washburn, "The Study of Race." Presidential Address to the American Anthropological Association, November 16, 1962, in *The Concept of Race*, ed. Ashley Montagu (Glencoe, Ill.: The Free Press, 1964), 242-60.

6. Lancelot Hogben, "The Race Concept," in *The Concept of Race*, ed. Ashley Montagu (Glencoe, Ill.: The Free Press, 1964), 86-102. It is coincidental that Hogben was Professor Emeritus at Birmingham University in 1960 when he published the lines cited.

7. Although it appears to accomplish little, objective analysts seem obsessively repetitive in their assessment of evidence that the concept of race is a fiction created to benefit certain interests during the colonial era. Scott L. Malcomson provides a recent example in his *One Drop of Blood: The American Misadventure of Race* (New York: Farrar, Straus, Giroux, 2000).

8. Marshall Segal, "How We Talk about Race: Implications from the Human Genome Project" (address presented at a conference on International Perspective on Race, Ethnicity, and Intercultural Relations, University of Mississippi, Oxford, Miss., 19 April 2001).

9. William I. Thomas, *The Unadjusted Girl* (Boston: Little, Brown & Company, 1923).

10. Graham C. Kinloch, *The Comparative Understanding of Intergroup Relations: A Worldwide Analysis* (Boulder, Colo: Westview Press, 1999).

11. Edward Shils, "Color, the Universal Intellectual Community, and the Afro-Asian Intellectual," *Daedalus* (spring 1967): 279-95.

12. Zevi is quoted by Victor L. Simpson, *Washington Post*, 29 December 1990, 7(B).

13. Roger Bastide, "Color, Race, and Christianity," *Daedalus* (spring 1967): 312-27.

14. Brian Lavery, "Old Prejudice Lives on in a Multiracial Ireland," *New York Times*,

18 November 2001, 12 (A).

15. William Joyce, "Nomadism, Ethnicity, and the Traveller Community: An Irish Case Study" (comments as a panelist at the International Conference on Racial Equality in Europe, Birmingham, England, 5 December 1991).

16. The resolutions of those groups were issued on 7 January 1992 and transmitted through several electronic networks. The set of resolutions can be obtained from KUNA, Via Espana, Edif. Brasilia Piso 1, Oficina 9-A, Apartado Postal 536. Panama 1, PANAMA.

17. I was reminded by my daughter Martha of Shakespeare as both a source and a reflection of popular imagery at that time.

18. Pitt-Rivers, "Race, Color, and Class."

19. Charles Hirschman,"Ethnic Blending in Historicial Perspective" (paper presented at the annual meetings of The American Sociological Association. Cincinnati, Ohio, August 1991).

20. Robert G. Cushing, "Review of *Cultural Identity and Ethnicity in the Pacific*," *Contemporary Sociology* (May 1991): 356-57.

21. James Rupert, "Central Asia Faces Struggle over Future," *Washington Post*, 19 December 1991, 41(A).

22. Blaine Hardin, "Some Say Bosnia Fight Not Ethnic," *Washington Post*, 14 June 1992.

23. James Rupert and Steven Coll, "Ethnic Rivalries Resurface in Afghan Coalition Council," *Washington Post*, 2 April 1992, 1(A).

24. Luc Gauthier and Amalia Fawcett, "How Does National Identity Emerge or How the Maori and Quebec Cultures Survived and Prospered in Spite of History" (paper presented at a conference, International Perspectives on Race, Ethnicity, and Intercultural Relations, University of Mississippi, Oxford, Mississippi., 21 April 2001).

25. Jocelyn Linnekin and Lin Poyer, eds., *Cultural Identity and Ethnicity in the Pacific* (Honolulu: University of Hawaii Press, 1990).

26. Catherine Newbury, *The Cohesion of Oppression: Clientship and Ethnicity in Rwanda 1860-1960* (New York: Columbia University Press, 1988).

27. Bob Blauner, "Racism, Race, and Ethnicity: Some Reflections on the Language of Race" (paper presented at the annual meeting of the American Sociological Association, Cincinnati, Ohio, 23 August 1991).

28. Joel Achenbach, "Columbus Rediscovered," *Washington Post*, 14 July 1991, 4(F) and 5(F).

29. Dan Pavel, "Romania's Hidden Victims: Wanderers," *New Republic* (4 March 1991), 12-13.

30. Samantha Power, "Bystanders to Genocide," *The Atlantic Monthly* (September 2001). Four additional cases are proposed by Cocker: The Germans in South West Africa (Namibia) in 1904, the American war against the Apaches, the Spanish in Mexico, and— the most effective of all—the complete annihilation of the aborigines in Tasmania by the British. See Mark Cocker, *Rivers of Blood, Rivers of Gold: Europe's Conquest of Indigenous People"* New York: Grove, 2000).

31. George Will, *Washington Post*, 21 June, 1990.

32. Long Litt Woon, "The European Tribe: A Question of Identity," in *RacialEquality in Europe: Conference Report*, ed. Khurshid Ahmed (Birmingham, England: Birmingham City Council Race Relations Unit, 1993), 27.

33. *Asiaweek*, "Strangers In Their Native Land," (4 May 1990) 18-20.

34. Long Litt Woon, "The European Tribe," 28.

35. E. Robinson, *Washington Post*, 23 June 1991. In the same vein as *mestizo* is the emerging image—the new ethnic identity in the Carribean—called *creolite* (see Debra Anderson, "Beyond 'Antillanite'/In Praise of 'Creolite': History and Identity in Francophone Literature from the Caribbean" [paper presented at a Symposium, Rediscovering America: 1492-1992, Louisiana State University, Baton Rouge, Louisiana, 27 February 1992]). Such blended ethnics can also find themselves referred to in pejorative terms such as the "Anglo-Indian." For essays dealing with nine such peoples throughout the world see Noel P. Gist and Anthony Gary Dworkin, eds., *The Blending of Races: Marginality and Identity in World Perspective* (New York: John Wiley & Sons, 1972).

36. Julia Preston, "Brazil Grants Land Rights to Indians," *Washington Post*, 16 November 1991, 24(A).

37. This news was received electronically over the ANTHAP listserve on 14 January 1992. Its source is the Nucleus for Indigenous Rights, which brought suit on behalf of the Indians: Nucleo de Direitos Indigenas SCS Q 06 BL A. Ed. Jose Severo sla 303 Cep 703000, Brasilia, DF BRAZIL.

38. William Claiborne, "Canada, Eskimos to Create Vast Arctic Territory," *Washington Post*, 17 December 1991.

Chapter 4

Identities: Ethnic and Otherwise

I am sure I shall enjoy visiting Ireland one year soon, and I may even go to County Armaugh and look at the church records in the little town my great grandfather came from. Or look up the British records from the people who wanted to hang him. But man I don't want to live there! Jesus, you think I'm freaking *nuts*? I'm *American* and damned glad to be too. If I have a tribe, they wear red, white, and blue tattoos.

— Reece McGee, sailor, sociologist, poet, and farmer

By 1966 troubling events were beginning to occur in Vietnam and the American civil rights movement led by Martin Luther King was fading. In chapter 1, I told how I found myself in a public debate at Syracuse University awkwardly defending King's unpopular dream of a world no longer populated by white people or black people but by fully assimilated brown people. Both King and his dream were on the wane. My adversary, you remember, was one of a new breed of leaders—an angry and articulate Stokely Carmichael who urged Negroes to take pride in their African heritage. He was persuasive enough to shake my integrationist and assimilationist convictions. I felt sadly uncertain about King's (and my own) vision. I was saddened by the awareness that *as long as one group defines itself as collectively "different" from another group, that difference will become an invidious one.* Nevertheless, Carmichael was instrumental in a resurgence of pride of ancestry and culture among many American ethnic groups. Perhaps the American melting pot had never existed. Or, perhaps we were "beyond the melting pot."[1] Well, perhaps we were and then again perhaps we were not. That issue will be resolved in chapter 13.

With the publication in 1942 of *Man's Most Dangerous Myth*, Ashley Montagu effectively laid to rest earlier claims of biological and genetic bases for racial and ethnic identity. He not only documented the largely colonial origins of such fictional identities but also the manner of their imposition and their disruptive social consequences. With the passage of a half-century it is becoming increasingly clear that the assumption of ethnic or racial identity is shifting in many cases from resistence to prideful and purposeful adoption. The next chapter focuses on three cases exhibiting this resurgence of ethnic identity. It was stimulated by a reading of Montagu's sixth edition, which appeared in 1997.[2]

Montagu's first edition of 1942 was inspired by the atrocities in ideology and behavior committed by the Nazis in the name of what they called their racial superiority. His meticulous assembly and assessment of biological research put the idea of physical racial categories to rest, including those of his colleagues in physical anthropology, who, in the 1940s, were classifying humanity into endless categories of species and subspecies. In fact Carleton Coon was at it well into the 1960s.[3]

Since those early years Montagu increasingly fashioned his evidence into a revealing exposure of American racial attitudes and behaviors. The major revision in his 1997 edition is a new chapter in which he disposes of Herrnstein and Murray's *The Bell Curve* as "a massive manifestation of genteel bigotry."[4] Montagu's legacy should have been to lay to rest forever what he called the myth of race. But, as we know, scientific evidence and rational arguments are not the defining characteristics of the contemporary world. Montagu understood this sad truth too. He appears to have independently discovered W. I. Thomas's "Definition of the Situation":

> Feelings and thoughts concerning such a concept as race are real enough, and so, it may be pointed out, are feelings and thoughts concerning the existence of unicorns, pixies, goblins, satyrs, ghosts, Jews, blacks, Catholics, and foreigners in general.[5]

Later on the same page he reminds us: "The lesson necessary for all of us to understand and learn is that *the meaning of a word is the action it produces.* No matter if words and beliefs are false, if men define them as real, they will be real in their consequences."

As important as Montagu's work is, he seems to have failed to foresee, and does not incorporate into it, the new wave of racial and ethnic pride which has swept the United States. This movement has stood on its head some of the arguments concerning the evils of the idea of race which Montagu equates with "caste" and which he hopes will be replaced by ethnicity.[6] Although he recognizes the cultural basis for some ethnic group identities (and clearly respects what he views as the richness of a culturally diverse society), the fact is that race for him is nothing more than caste, an evil hierarchical ranking of fictional groups into superior and inferior ones.

Montagu is convinced that, through education and socialization, the idea of race, which is imposed upon minorities and serves as a basis for scapegoating, can eventually be purged from society. The three cases discussed in the next chapter all suggest a radically different process: *a deliberate effort on the part of a minority to create or re-create a racial or ethnic identity.*

The Rebirth of Ethnic Pride

This rebirth of ethnic pride can have curious consequences. An ageing colleague of mine tells of visiting a gathering in which people were asked to identify themselves. One young woman announced, "I am a sociologist." She paused and then continued: "and I am an Italian American." My friend, an Italian American of two generations earlier was shocked and recalled how he and his fellow Italian American college students did their best in the 1940s and 1950s to disguise their ethnicity. They would have been embarrassed, but here was a young person of the 1990s proudly announcing her ethnic origins.

The evidence is more than anecdotal that something happened in the interim between these generations. Salmaone[7] notes that in thirteen of the leading textbooks of anthropology from 1919 to 1971 there were no index listings for "ethnic" or "ethnic group." Recall that when I informed my students in Calcutta that the melting pot was not fashionable in the United States at the moment, they thought I was joking. The fact is that it is not. They listened in disbelief when I discussed some of the origins and rationales for contemporary American multiculturalism. The selfsame Nathan Glazer who announced with Moynihan in 1963 that the melting pot had never existed, proclaims in 1993 that even the word "'assimilation' is not today a popular term."[8] But, aware that fashions are transient affairs which easily succumb to time, I urged the Indian students to be patient. And, in fact by 1997 Alba and Nee had the temerity to suggest that, although the term "assimilation" was in bad repute, "assimilation theory has not lost its utility [for research purposes]."[9] As the new millennium approached, other sociologists began to publish research more boldly suggesting that assimilation was proceeding at a rapid rate. We shall consider their evidence in chapter 13.

It is arguable that social scientists reflect the shifting fashions of the larger society in their social analyses. One of the most popular American textbooks on intergroup relations in the late 1960s and early 1970s bore the title *Assimilation in American Life*.[10] By the mid-1970s, *The Rise of the Unmeltable Ethnics*[11] had become a necessary reference and one of the more popular textbooks bore the title *Cultural Pluralism*.[12] By 1981 the Gordon of assimilation fame had edited a volume entitled *America as A Multicultural Society*.[13] One columnist notes a certain irony in contemporary intergroup ideology:

> The irony is that a few decades ago the liberal agenda was based on the belief that people were similar and deserving of equal rights regardless of their skin color or national origin or religion. Now the liberal agenda, or at least the multiculturalist appendix, requires that everyone be labeled by race, ethnicity, sex, economic

status, sexual preference, religion, etc. Everyone can thereby be categorized as either oppressor or oppressed. Who you are matters less than what you are.[14]

Echoing Achenbach, the conservative *Boston Globe* columnist David Warsh describes the Ethnic Heritage Studies Program act of 1974 as "a congressional act that, while little noted nor long remembered seems to sum up all of the arrogance of the cult of ethnicity."[15] Strangely, Arthur Schlesinger, Jr., a liberal servant of the Democratic Party,is in complete agreement. He believes that same act "compromised the historical right of Americans to decide their ethnic identities for themselves."[16] It seems that not all liberals have abandoned the liberal agenda of a few decades ago as Achenbach suggests. In chapter 5 we will encounter some Americans (Italian Americans and Native Americans) who are in fact exercising what Schlesinger calls their historical right to decide their ethnic identities for themselves.

The ideological chasm is not as clear a divide as some would have us believe. In 1991, Schlesinger published a passionate appeal for a return to assimilationist values. He asks if the worldwide ethnic upheaval which dismembers Yugoslavia, strains the former U.S.S.R., and endangers Canada, will also tribalize America. Will it, he asks, turn us into a bunch of squabbling nationalities? This "cult of ethnicity," Schlesinger insists, threatens the original American ideal of one people—*e pluribus unum*. For him the problem is "how to restore the balance between *unum* and *pluribus*?"[17]

If liberal and conservative ideologies become confused on this issue, so too does the distinction between the detached scholar and the ideologue. Witness the attack by an eminent sociologist on a colleague who had reviewed favorably a set of books suggesting that early-twentieth-century Chicago theories of assimilation discussed in chapter 13 seem to be supported by contemporary research. Adopting the rhetoric of the far right, Greeley accuses Hirschman of being "politically correct" and subscribing to a "neoassimilationist ideology."[18] Greeley[19] angrily rebukes Hirschman for failing to take note of his own (Greeley's) research which indicates that we do indeed live in an increasingly pluralistic society. If all of this appears to dwell on the petty differences among academics, it does not. It is shifting fashions and ideology which are coming into play.

The fact that Greeley employs language favored by the ideological right in its attack on multiculturalism lends additional confusion since Greeley is a strong proponent of a culturally pluralist society. A solution to this issue is proposed by another scholar. In a sense Waxman has is both ways. He distinguishes between his ideological preference and his knowledge of the empirical evidence. While acknowledging that he is an ideological pluralist, Waxman reluctantly calls himself an empirical assimilationist: "the empirical assimilationist is one who, regardless of his own personal ideology and hopes, foresees, on the basis of his interpretation of the empirical evidence, the ultimate assimilation of large segments of the American Jewish population."[20]

Although it may be historically imprecise, I would date the shift from a melting pot image of America to an ethnically diverse one to Stokely Carmichael's rallying cry of "black is beautiful" beginning around 1960.[21] Shortly afterward, the cry could be read in a rash of bumper stickers and buttons declaring, "Polish is beautiful," "Kiss me I'm Irish," "Italian Power" and, in honor of the quincentenary, "Leif made it first." Eisenstadt dates "the weakening ideology of the melting pot and the upsurge of ethnic pride in general," as "beginning in the late 1950s."[22] Carmichael, I believe, played a critical role in the rebirth of overt ethnic pride in the United States. In 1963 Glazer and Moynihan provided the academic underpinning for that rebirth: *Beyond the Melting Pot*[23] is an elegant analysis of research dealing with New York City's "Negroes, Puerto Ricans, Jews, Italians and Irish." It was also a timely, if inappropriate, justification for the rediscovery of ethnic identity. That seriously flawed study is important enough to merit some consideration.

As excellent as their research may be as a comparative study of certain ethnic groups in New York City at a particular moment in history, there is nothing in the Glazer and Moynihan book to justify their statement: "The notion that the intense and unprecedented mixture of ethnic and religious groups in American life was soon to blend into a homogeneous end product has outlived its usefulness, and also its credibility."[24]

They qualify their statement that the melting pot did not happen: "At least not in New York and, *mutis mutandis* in those parts of America which resemble New York."[25] This claim in the preface is followed by an introductory chapter which persuasively develops the thesis that New York is different from other American cities. Not only is it difficult to generalize from this study, but it is in fact an analysis of a distorted sample of immigrants and their descendants: these are the ghettoized residues of the millions who passed through New York and left those ghettoes behind along with their ethnic identities. Alba and Nee remind us: "There is abundant evidence that assimilation has been the master trend among the descendants of the immigrants of the previous era of mass immigration, who mainly came from Europe in the period before 1930."[26] New York City may indeed have been a conveyer belt to assimilation—a belt on which some immigrants were either unable or unwilling to climb. Ultimately Glazer and Moynihan concede that groups do disappear. They acknowledge that in New York "Germans as a group are vanished" and that "Germans have been assimilated."[27]

In one of their tables Glazer and Moynihan summarize the population of New York by race and ethnicity between the years 1900 and 1960. But they inform us that these figures "assume that everyone in the city can be neatly assigned to an ethnic category. Of course this is in large measure myth; many of the people in the city as in the nation, have parents and grandparents of two or three or four [ethnic] groups."[28] This seems to me to be evidence of considerable assimilation. In fact Glazer and Moynihan appear to agree with Robert E. Park, founder of the Chicago School, that ethnic labels will be "erased in America":

"This may still be the most likely result *in the long run*."[29] They are concerned that the "notion of an American Melting pot did not . . . grasp what would happen in the short run, and since this short run encompasses at least the length of a normal lifetime, it is not something we can ignore."[30] I am unaware of anyone suggesting that the melting pot would occur in "the length of a normal lifetime." As we shall see in chapters 9 and 13, there is a continuous chain of evidence (beginning at the turn of the last century and running into the turn of this one) that it takes about three generations for the assimilation process to run its course.

Glazer and Moynihan reflect the parochial worldview of New Yorkers who, like Parisians, often assume that their own limited horizon somehow typifies their nation. They believe that there is "a satisfaction in being with those who are like oneself. The ethnic group is something of an extended family or tribe."[31] There are authorities in this field who view such tribalism as the core of intergroup problems. At the close of this chapter we will return to the concept of "extensivity" which suggests a cure for tribalism.

In sum, this shift in fashion toward a rediscovery of ethnic pride began to gain momentum in the 1960s. Thanks in large part to Stokely Carmichael and his confederates the thrust toward diversity began to overwhelm the beginnings of racial integration. Other events followed swiftly. Glazer and Moynihan provided an intellectual rationale with their argument that the melting pot had never been more than a romantic illusion. The Ethnic Studies Program Act was passed in 1974 with its emphasis on nurturing cultural diversity. Alex Haley's popular novel *Roots* was published in 1976 and became a television series the following year. *Roots* kindled a national interest in searching out the ancestral past, with its national and ethnic origins.[32] With the advent of the Reagan-Bush years came the angry conservative reaction to affirmative action, multiculturalism, multilingual education, and other pluralist policies. The first president Bush resisted all civil rights legislation for several years on the often spurious ground that it involved quotas. Some of the rhetoric of this period was mentioned earlier along with the observation that segments of the liberal left, if not angry, were certainly disappointed in the new intergroup fashions.

But fashion is a fickle process and there is some evidence that, at least among scholars, its finger may be moving on in a direction that should please my students in Calcutta. By the mid-1990s, writers like Hirschman and Alba no longer appeared to be, at best anachronisms, or, at worst, tools of conservative xenophobes. They had strengthened their theoretical positions and had become part of a new stream of assimilationist literature. Alba and Nee announce, "We are not alone in this attempt."[33] They cite Barkan,[34] Kazal,[35] and Morowska[36] as examples of scholars who keep them company.

How Important Is Ethnicity?

Students of ethnicity sometimes forget that one's identity has many components of which ethnicity is only one. Is it safe to assume that it is always the salient one? This brief review of events, which seem to me to account for the rebirth of ethnic pride, needs some qualification. There is considerable evidence that in the United States, especially among European Americans, this pride may have occurred without any concomitant rebirth of ethnicity itself. Glazer and Moynihan, however, take their own data seriously:

> If one believes, as the authors of this book do, that the distinctions [among ethnic groups] are important, and that they consist of more than the amusing differences of accent and taste in food and drink, then it is no simple matter to decide how to describe and analyze this aspect of American reality.[37]

Those "amusing differences" would later become the subject of serious analysis by Herbert Gans who refers to them as "symbolic ethnicity."[38] This is precisely what is described in a study of Armenian-Americans in New York and New Jersey. These people continue to take pride in their ethnic origins but according to Bakalian, "for most Armenian-Americans, Armenianness is food, hospitality, and generosity."[39] Much the same thing is found among three generations of Germans, Italians, Jews, and Ukrainians in contemporary Toronto.[40] And in a comparative review of two American studies, Hirschman concludes: "Ethnicity did not determine one's career, marriage partner, friends, or neighborhood, but was an interesting extra to spice up life."[41] In his book *Italian Americans*, Alba writes of "expressive" ethnic identity: parades, cooking, festivals, and other occasions when members play at being "ethnic."[42]

Among the descendants of European immigrants in the United States, considerable assimilation has occurred. Ethnicity may indeed have become largely symbolic. In fact, by late 1991, Glazer appears to have altered his conclusions that the melting pot never happened and that it is important to maintain distinctions among ethnic groups. Now, like Schlessinger, he takes "issue with the attempt to turn the United States into a congeries of ethnic and racial groups, and nothing more. Assimilation is a reality: scores of millions of unhyphenated Americans, who owe no allegiance to any identity other than American, are evidence of that."[43]

If then, there is some evidence that American ethnic identity may be superficial, there is also a bit of evidence that, among all possible identities, the ethnic one may not always be salient. It is true that urban sophisticates in Sarajevo could in the 1980s intermarry extensively and, by and large, treat their ethnic origins as irrelevant:

> Baros [a Serb], his Muslim wife and their friends in the living room are an ethnic hodgepodge typical of this capital and other large towns in Bosnia-Hercegovina.

> There on the ottoman sits a Muslim marketing man married to a Jewish literature professor. Standing beside the overgrown philodendron is a Croat restauranteur who would rather be called a Yugoslav. . . . 'We are all city kids here. Growing up, we called each other by silly nicknames. Until two months ago, we didn't even know each other's religion.'[44]

Bringa, who studied nòt urban folk but isolated villagers, reports much the same thing although she suggests a greater awareness of ethnicity among country people. She reports that "difference in ethnoreligious affiliation was one of the many differences between people, like differences between men and women, villager and city dweller. It was acknowledged and often joked about but it never precluded friendship. "Indeed," she continues, "for these Bosnians being Bosnian (*bosanac*) meant growing up in a multicultural and multireligious environment, an environment where cultural pluralism was intrinsic to the social order."[45]

It is also true that German Jews could, in the 1920s, come to think of themselves as Germans more than as Jews, but as both instances tragically illustrate, dominant groups do not always permit minorities to shed that identity.[46] Yet there are bits of evidence, from both contemporary history and contemporary sociology, suggesting that ethnic identity does not necessarily maintain priority when people have other choices. The research evidence, preliminary though it may be, is based upon a Malaysian study in which interview respondents are provided with choices of loyalties under different conditions. The study attempts to determine the criteria by which people chose to align themselves with others. "It [the research] offers support for the view that economic development in Malaysia has been giving rise to situations in which Malay-Chinese interactions are governed in whole or part by non-ethnic norms."[47]

Confirmation is found in anecdotal evidence from India. An effort on the part of poor women to ban the sale of cheap government-produced liquor appears to override religious and caste concerns:

> United by a common cause, high caste and lower caste village women who previously never would have shared a meal overcame traditional prejudice to work side by side. In one village, when police tried to accuse Sikhs involved in the protest movement of being terrorists, Hindu villagers raced to their defense. In many areas, Hindus and Muslims jointly shut down liquor shops.[48]

In the Malaysian instance, it is economic interactions which take precedence over ethnic ones and in the Indian case it is a social reform which transcends ethnicity. Ronald Cohen views this phenomenon as "situational ethnicity," varying with the context of the social situation.[49] There is some hint of this process among young second-generation Bangladeshis in London's East End. The interviews reported by Eade reflect considerable shifting of identity in terms of reference groups: family, English people, Muslims, etc. But "there is also a tendency to rank the identities."[50] Having spent some time among anthropology students and faculty in Calcutta, who seemed to think of themselves more as

Bengalis than Indians, I was struck by the salience of the Bengali identity among Eade's Bangladeshi immigrants. Clearly nationality is not always a central identity.

This notion of situational identity has somewhat different implications from the hierarchical one. Slavenka Drakulic describes such nonhierarchical multiple identities as they appear among the peoples of Istria, a Croatian peninsula at the juncture of Croatia, Slovenia, and Italy. She tells us that in Istria, the "mixture of languages and the ease with which the people slip from one into the other is characteristic of life here." People, she writes, do not make problems out of their differences; it is others who do that:

> When in 1994 a Croat reporter interviewed inhabitants of three Croatian border villages which had been annexed overnight by Slovenes, he was faced with a "strange" reaction. To the Croat reporter, these people said that they were Croats, to Italian reporters that they were, of course, Italians, and the Slovene reporters were told they were Slovenes. . . . The locals saw no contradiction in claiming three different nationalities; neither would they describe themselves as opportunists. In their view, the misunderstanding lies in the fact that the journalists were posing a simple "either-or" type of question. . . . The villagers were talking about their own identity, of which their nationalities were only one aspect. . . . [Istrians] want to avoid defining themselves or being defined by others as "pure" Croats, or Italians, or Slovenes, or Serbs. . . . To Istrians identity is broader and deeper than nationality. . . . They understand better than anyone else that we all have mixed blood to a greater or lesser extent.[51]

We have seen the wheel of fashion—both popular and scientific—turn from assimilation to pluralism and back to assimilation. We have also seen that even though ethnicity is salient to some people, there is evidence that (1), sometimes ethnicity may be viewed as "amusing differences" and (2), sometimes other affiliations and interests may supersede ethnic identity. Although Ashley Montagu might disapprove of the first, he would surely be pleased by the second possibility. In the next chapter we pursue this matter further by examining three cases of the resurgence of ethnic identity—or in contemporary parlance, peoples who have reinvented themselves.

Notes

1. Nathan Glazer and Daniel Patrick Moynihan, *Beyond the Melting Pot: The Negroes, Puerto Ricans, Jews, Italians, and Irish of New York City* (Cambridge, Mass.: M.I.T. Press, 1963). A brief but informative account of the notion of the melting pot from Crevecouer's 1782 observation that "Here individuals of all nations are melted into a new race" to Israel Zangwill's 1908 play "The Melting Pot" can be found on pages 288-91 in Glazer and Moynihan.

2. Ashley Montagu, *Man's Most Dangerous Myth: The Fallacy of Race*, 6th ed., Edition, abridged student edition (Walnut Creek, Calif.: Alta Mira Press, 1997).

3. Carleton S. Coon, *The Origin of Races* (New York: Knopf, 1962) and (with Edward E. Hunt) *The Living Races of Man* (New York: Knopf, 1965).

4. The quote appears on page 19 in the foreword by C. Loring Brace without attribution. The critique is of Richard J Herrnstein and Charles Murray, *The Bell Curve: Intelligence and Class Structure in American Life* (New York: The Free Press, 1994). Herrinstein and Murray are adherents of a long recurring tradition which consists of "scientific" demonstration of the relationship between physical characteristics and social behavior. That tradition ranges at least from the nineteenth-century Italian criminologist Caesare Lombroso, who showed how head shape could predict not only criminality but also the type of crime likely to be committed. Lombroso and his latter day imitators appear in chapter 5.

5. Montagu, *Man's Most Dangerous Myth*, 176.

6. I am not the only scholar to refuse to get bogged down in definitional trivia. Nagel says, "I use the terms 'American Indian'. . .[and] 'Native American'. . . interchangeably. . . . I also use the terms 'race' and 'ethnicity' somewhat interchangeably, although I view ethnicity as the broader concept." (See Joane Nagel, "American Indian Ethnic Renewal: Politics and the Resurgence of Identity," *American Sociological Review*, 60 [December 1995]: 947, n1). Alba and Nee in their extensive review of assimilation theory take the same position (See Richard D. Alba and Victor Nee, "Rethinking Assimilation Theory for a New Era of Immigration," *International Migration* Review 31[winter 1997]: 834, n2). For an example of how messy that bog can get see Fred W.Riggs, "Ethnicity, Nationalism, Race, Minority: A Semantic/Onomantic Exercise (Part One)" *International Sociology* 6, 3 (September 1991): 281-305. Part 2 appears in *International Sociology* 6, 4 (December 1991): 443-63.

7. Frank A. Salmaone, "Deciding Who 'We' Are: The Order of the Sons of Italy and the Creation of Italian-American Ethnicity," *Journal of Human and Environmental Science*, 1, 1 (spring 1996): 1-23.

8. Nathan Glazer, "Is Assimilation Dead?" *The Annals*, 530 (November 1993): 122-23.

9. Richard Alba and Victor Nee, "Rethinking Assimilation Theory," 826.

10. Milton M.Gordon, *Assimilation in American Life: The Role of Race, Religion, and National Origin* (New York: Oxford University Press, 1964).

11. R. D. Novak, *The Rise of the Unmeltable Ethnics* (New York: Macmillan, 1972).

12. M. Crawford Young, *Cultural Pluralism* (Madison: University of Wisconsin Press, 1977).

13. Milton M Gordon, ed., *America as a Multicultural Society*, special issue of *The Annals*, 454 (March 1981).

14. Joel Achenbach, "Columbus Rediscovered," *Washington Post*, 14 July 1991, 4(F)-5(F).

15. David Warsh, "Republicans Hold the High Ground by Embracing Melting Pot Ideal," reprinted from the *Boston Globe* in *Washington Post*, 6 November 1991, 3(C).

16. Arthur M. Schlesinger, Jr., *The Disuniting of America: Reflections on a Multicultural Society* (New York: W. W. Norton, 1991), 43.

17. Schlesinger, *The Disuniting of America*, 42-43, 133.

18. Charles Hirschman, "What Happened to the White Ethnics?" *Contemporary Sociology* 20, 2 (March 1991): 180-83.

19. Andrew Greeley, "Commentary," *Contemporary Sociology* 20, 3 (July 1991): 505.

20. Chaim I. Waxman, "Is the Cup Half-Full or Half-Empty? Perspectives on the Future of the American Jewish Community," in *American Pluralism and the Jewish Community*, ed. Seymour Martin Lipset (New Brunswick, N.J.: Transaction Publishers, 1990), 83, n6.

21. Stokely Carmichael and Charles V. Hamilton, *Black Power: The Politics of Liberation in America* (New York: Vintage Books, 1967). Carmichael's rallying cry was more likely "Black Power," but it is the "beautiful" dimension that contributed heavily to the resurrection of ethnic pride among the grandchildren of European immigrants and to a degree among Native Americans.

22. Shmuel Eisenstadt, "The American Jewish Experience and American Pluralism," in *American Pluralism and the Jewish Community,* ed. Seymour Martin Lipset, (New Brunswick, N.J.: Transaction Press, 1990), 43-52.

23. Nathan Glazer and Daniel Patrick Moynihan, *Beyond the Melting Pot.* The immigrant process as it was observed at the turn of the last century in American cities such as New York and Chicago, is repeating itself at the turn of the present century in Los Angeles. The "ethnics" are Asian and Hispanic rather than European but the processes are identical (the immigrant press, ethnic neighborhoods, interethnic hostilities, control over public jobs, ethnic trades, up and out migration to gilded ghettos or integrated communities for the more successful, etc.). For considerable data, along with some misinterpretations, see Michael A. Fletcher, "The Myth of the Melting Pot: America's Racial and Ethnic Divides," *Washington Post,* 7 April 1998, 1(A) and 4-5(A).

24. Glazer and Moynihan, *Beyond the Melting Pot,* v.

25. Glazer and Moynihan, *Beyond the Melting Pot,* v.

26. Alba and Nee, "Rethinking Assimilation," 841.

27. Glazer and Moynihan, *Beyond the Melting Pot,* 311.

28. Glazer and Moynihan, *Beyond the Melting Pot,* 9.

29. Glazer and Moynihan, *Beyond the Melting Pot,* 12-13 (italics added).

30. Glaser and Moynihan, *Beyond the Melting Pot,* 13.

31. Glaser and Moynihan, *Beyond the Melting Pot,* 18, 32. Their analysis of the role of politics in American ethnic identity provides one example: what they describe on pp. 301-10 is a truly local history of New York City of no relevance to any other place or time. Other examples of parochialism are abundant in this volume. It is unlikely that Glazer and Moynihan would have considered southern culture as relevant to their problem. Yet, there is extensive documentation that this is "where the pot truly melted." See, for example, Margaret Jones Bolsterli, "Southern Culture: The True Melting Pot" (paper delivered at a symposium, Rediscovering America: 1492-1992. Louisiana State University, Baton Rouge, Louisiana, 27 February 1992).

32. Alex Haley, *Roots* (New York: Doubleday, 1976). Schlesinger cites Sollors as claiming that if Haley had traced his father's rather than his mother's bloodline, "he would have traveled 12 generations back to, not Gambia, but Ireland." See Schlesinger, *The Disuniting of America,* 85, and Werner Sollors, *The Invention of Ethnicity* (New York: College Humanities and Social Sciences, 1991), 227.

33. Alba and Nee, "Rethinking Assimilation Theory," 827.

34. E. Barkan, "Race, Religion, and Nationality in American Society: A Model of Ethnicity–From Contact to Assimilation, *Journal of American Ethnic History* 14 (1995): 38-101.

35. R. Kazal, "Revisiting Assimilation: The Rise, Fall, and Reappraisal of a Concept in American Ethnic History," *American Historical Review* 100 (1995): 437-72.

36. E. Morawska, "In Defense of the Assimilation Model," *Journal of American Ethnic History* 13 (1994): 76-87.

37. Glazer and Moynihan, *Beyond the Melting Pot,* 21.

38. Herbert Gans, "Symbolic Ethnicity: The Future of Ethnic Groups and Cultures," *Racial and Ethnic Studies* 2 (1979): 1-20.

39. Anny Bakalian,"From Being to Feeling Armenian: Assimilation and Identity among Armenian Americans" (paper presented at the annual meeting of the American Sociological Association, Cincinnati, Ohio, August 1991).

40. Wsevold W. Isajiwa and Momo Podolosky, "The Deconstruction and Reconstruc-

tion of Ethnicity in Culturally Diverse Societies" (paper presented at the annual meeting of the American Sociological Association, Cincinnati, Ohio, August 1991).

41. Charles Hirschman, "What Happened to the White Ethnics?" *Contemporary Sociology* 20.2 (March 1991): 180-83. The two studies compared were Richard D. Alba, *Ethnic Identity: The Transformation of White America* (New Haven, Conn.: Yale University Press 1990) and Mary C. Waters, *Ethnic Options: Choosing Identities in America* (Berkeley: University of California Press, 1990).

42. Richard D. Alba, *Italian-Americans* (Englewood Cliffs, N.J.: Prentice Hall, 1985).

43. Nathan Glazer, "Is Assimilation Dead?" *The Annals* 530 (November 1993) 122-36. This is a radical reversal of his position two years earlier in his "In Defense of Multiculturalism," *The New Republic* (2 September 1991): 18-22. He offers no explanation.

44. Blaine Hardin, "Some Say Bosnia Fight Not Ethnic," *Washington Post,* 14 June 1992, 28(A).

45. Tone Bringa, *Being Muslim the Bosnia Way: Identity and Community in a Central Bosnian Village* (Princeton, N. J.: Princeton University Press, 1995), 83.

46. Istvan Szabo's movie *Sunshine* (2000) implies that no matter what the minority does it is to no avail. Assimilation is impossible. The story follows three generations of Hungarian Jews through the twentieth century as Hungary finds itself under the rule of the Austro-Hungarian Empire, Nazi Germany, and finally the Soviet Union. All three generations fail in their efforts to become Hungarians rather than Jews.

47. Michael Banton and Mohd Noor Mansor, "The Study of Ethnic Alignment: A New Technique and an Application in Malaysia," *Ethnic and Racial Studies* 15 (4 October 1992): 612.

48. Molly Moore, "Indian Village Women Fight State, Husbands to Ban Liquor," *Washington Post*, 19 December 1993, 38(A).

49. Ronald Cohen, "Ethnicity: Problem and Focus in Anthropology," *Annual Review of Anthropology* 7 (1978): 379-403. Cited by Frank A. Salmaone, "Deciding Who 'We' Are," 3-4.

50. John Eade, "Identity, Nation and Religion: Educated Young Bangladeshi Muslims in London's 'East End,'" *International Sociology* 9 (September 1994): 386.

51. Slavenka Drakulik, *Café Europa* (New York: W. W. Norton, 1997), 163-64.

Chapter 5

Ethnic Renewal: Italian Americans, Bosnian Muslims, and Native Americans

> Ethnicity is strong medicine. A little can improve the quality of
> life; large doses can kill us.
>
> —Milton Yinger, *Ethnicity: Social Strength, Social Conflict*
> (New York: State University of New York Press, 1994) 150

It was a balmy afternoon in the spring of 1998. I was in a resort hotel in San Juan, Puerto Rico, addressing a collection of applied anthropologists on the subject of ethnic identity. I had recently run across research on Italian Americans, Native Americans, and Bosnian Muslims which I thought had a common theme. This chapter reviews my attempt to bring coherence to that chaos. As Yinger suggests, ethnicity may be a good thing and then again it may not.

Explaining the title of his book *The Lexus and the Olive Tree*, Thomas Friedman writes: "Olive trees are what give us the warmth of family, the joy of individuality, the intimacy of personal rituals, the depths of private relationships." At their best, according to Friedman, "they provide the feeling of self-esteem and belonging that are as essential for human survival as food in the belly."

> At worse, though, when taken to excess, an obsession with our olive trees
> leads us to forge identities, bonds, and communities based on the exclusion
> of others, and at their very worst, when these obsessions really run amok, as
> with the Nazis in Germany or the Serbs in Yugoslavia, they lead to the
> extermination of others.[1]

The instances considered in this chapter reflect a resurgent ethnicity—"ethnic renewal" as Nagel calls it: "Ethnic renewal is the reconstruction of one's ethnic identity by reclaiming a discarded identity, replacing or amending an identity in an existing ethnic identity repertoire, or filling a personal ethnic void."[2] On the one hand each of the three groups considered in this chapter has had its identity imposed by a powerful ethnic other, but on the other hand each identity is accompanied by a sense of collective and individual pride in that ethnicity.

Furthermore, each of these groups is experiencing its ethnicity in a different way for a second time—thus the terms "renewal" or "resurgence." In all three cases, the current ethnic identity replaces a previous one. In contrast to their similarities, however, each ethnic group is vastly different from the other two and each was formed under circumstances different from the other two.

Italian Americans

In spite of the pride taken by the young sociologist in chapter 3 who identifies herself as an Italian American, her grandparents may not have been aware of the hyphenated ethnicity and probably had no concept of ever having been Italian. Although all three cases are instances of the creation of ethnic identity by the minority itself in response to labeling by the dominant group, the Italian-American case is the most dramatic illustration of this process. Salmaone reminds us that "immigrants from the new country of Italy had to learn to be Italians." His article focuses on the role of the Order of the Sons of Italy in America (OSIA) in forging the Italian-American ethnic identity. "The immigrants which OSIA helped organize most frequently did not identify themselves as Italians. They identified themselves in terms of the smallest unit of identification possible in reference to the person who asked them what they were." He reminds us that "Each person owed loyalty to family, *paese* [community], and *regione*. Italy was a new country."[3]

Having had an ethnic identity created for them, Italian Americans were in a better position to compete for American opportunities with those immigrant groups who had preceded them and those who would follow them. Although a few quaint "Little Italies" remained in American cities to protect the elderly and unsuccessful and to feed and entertain tourists, Italian Americans were largely assimilated into American society by the end of the Second World War.

Salmaone is aware of the various ethnic "power movements" which began to emerge in the late 1960s and suggests that ethnic renewal among Italians was more than symbolic because assimilation was far from complete:

> In the 1960s many Italian-Americans who paid little attention to their heritage other than to attend an occasional opera, eat pasta, and visit their parents regularly began to discover that they were not truly accepted into the wider society. . . . In sum, they found that although prejudice and discrimination were more

subtle, they still existed and closed top positions to them.[4]

A study of the Irish in Albany, New York, helps to illuminate this phenomenon. Byron observes that in Albany, the Irish were welcomed by an extant German Catholic community.[5] Failing to encounter discrimination, they rapidly intermarried and assimilated. According to Byron, the descendants of Irish immigrants in Albany have no conception of themselves as Irish or as Irish American. He observes that this contrasts sharply with the Irish in Boston, New York, and Chicago where they encountered the same kinds of discrimination and prejudice Salmaone notes among the Italian immigrants. It comes as no surprise that minorities who are treated with respect by the dominant group rapidly assimilate while those who are treated with contempt cling to their ethnic identities. Evidence considered in parts 2 and 3 of this book leads precisely to that conclusion.

The young sociologist who proudly identified herself as Italian American in the 1990s is a product of the renewal of ethnic identity which blossomed after the civil rights movement of the 1960s and 1970s. Salmaone concentrates on the role of an ethnic organization in creating a collective sense of identity. This was necessary because "'Americans' lumped all Italians together."[6] This is the imposition of ethnic identity by outsiders who are ignorant of the peoples they stereotype. The dramatic instance of this ignorant imposition among my three cases is that of the Bosnian Muslims. This may seem strange since these people lived together with their labelers for centuries, but consider the images white America retains of African Americans and it no longer seems so strange.

Bosnian Muslims

Drakulic informs us that the Bosnian Muslims were given an official nationality in the mid-1970s in order to maintain the balance between Serbs and Croats in Bosnia. She also reminds us that Bosnian Muslims are of Slavic origin as are their Catholic (Croat) and Orthodox (Serbian) neighbors.[7] I would add to this the important commonality of language: all three groups spoke Serbo-Croatian as their first language. I use the past tense since both Serbs and Croats have, following the Bosnian war of the 1990s, made self-conscious efforts to alter their languages so that they better reflect the ethnicity of the speaker. Bringa explains that "the state defined Croats and Muslims (and Serbs) as distinct 'people' or 'nations' (narodi), but the locals also made the distinction between different nacije (religions). The Muslims thought highly of Tito because he gave them nationality status which gave them equal representation in all governmental bodies."[8]

It is clear that religion and nationality were of little relevance in the more sophisticated urban centers before the war, but it is also true that these things were far from central to the lives and personal identities of Bosnian villagers. Being Muslim seems to have served primarily to distinguish people from Croats and Serbs mainly for political purposes. In Bosnia, Muslims were more likely to identify themselves as Yugoslavs, atheists, and Communists than their more parochial Croat and Serb neighbors. The cultural traditions practiced by village Muslims were a melange of Islamic customs, Orthodox and Catholic holy days and feast days, and some pre-Christian practices.

One young Muslim cleric explained to the ethnographer Bringa that she would learn nothing of Muslim customs in the village she was studying because "They only do things the way they think it should be and their religion is mixed up with Christianity and all sorts of things."[9] It is my impression from Bringa's data that he was correct. For example, although religious education was provided for Muslim children, it was not taken very seriously. She reports that "*Mektab* ran parallel with primary school, that is, a child started at the age of six or seven and went on until the age of fourteen or fifteen. Most children, however, dropped out much earlier, and some children never attended as their parents did not mind."[10]

In the state schools "a 'Muslim' was a member of a primarily 'Yugoslav' *nacija*, that is, a communist and nonreligious."[11] There is no question but what these rural villages were far more traditional and conservative in their ways than the effete urban and suburbanites with whom they had frequent contact. That frequent contact, whether at work, during compulsory military service, or in state schools, was rapidly eroding the remnants of peasant life in Bosnia. Bringa reports that young women preparing for the bus ride into the city frequently changed their clothing (from long skirts to culottes) and arranged more sophisticated hairdos (doffing their headscarves) and put on makeup at the bus station or on the bus. Bosnia and Bosnians were, for better or for worse, on their way to becoming a modern urban society. That was before the war.

In the foreword to her book, written during the war and after the completion of her fieldwork, Bringa writes that the media coverage of the war painted two different images of the past: "The first is that the people of Bosnia-Hercegovina have always hated each other and whatever tolerance and coexistence there was had been imposed by the communist regime. The other is the idealized approach that Bosnia-Hercegovina, with its potent symbol Sarajevo, was the ideal example of a harmonious and tolerant multicultural society, where people did not classify each other in terms of 'Serb,' 'Muslim,' or 'Croat.'"[12] Neither of these conforms to her experience during the five years she lived there before the war broke out in 1992. I would suggest, however, that, good field-worker that she was, Bringa invested all of her time and energy in a rural village and that much of her reports of urban life are from the perspective of her rural informants. There is considerable evidence that the war was largely a class war, masked as an ethnoreligious one, between haves and have-nots, between educated and uneducated, between urban sophisticates and simple rural people.[13] I shall touch upon this again.

It was with the war in Bosnia that ethnic identity was violently imposed. If you did not have it you died. If you did have it you might survive. Drakulic allows that nobody should be killed because of the wrong ethnicity, "but it is an even bigger tragedy if people are killed because of what they are not." She goes on to say that this is what happened to the Bosnians: "They were ethnically cleansed at the beginning of the war on the pretext that they were religious Muslims, even fundamentalists. Of course this was not true." But when the violence against them began and when Europe failed to act, they turned to those who offered help. Drakulic puts it well: "If you are being killed as Muslim fundamentalists in spite of being a European, non-religious, Slavic people of Muslim nationality, and the only source of help were Muslim countries you would finally be forced to turn Muslim in order to survive."[14]

I think that Bringa reluctantly agrees: "The Bosnians," she writes, "have apparently been organized into tidy, culturally and ethnically homogeneous categories, and the Muslims seem finally to have become a neat ethno-national category its neighbors and the international community can deal with and understand. They have been forced by the war and the logic of the creation of nation-states to search for their origins and establish a 'legitimate' and continuous national history."[15] Drakulic refers to the "pushing of the Bosnian Muslims into the hands of fundamentalist Muslims from the Middle East" as an irreversible European mistake.[16]

So it is that a renewed and stronger sense of ethnicity can be imposed upon a people. Thanks to their Croat and Serb neighbors, Bosnians are now Muslims and Bosnia is a Muslim country. The cosmopolitan multiethnic Sarajevo, so romanticized by journalists and others in the mid-1990s, no longer exists. Sarajevo is a Muslim city. We have seen how Italian Americans could create their own new identity and how Muslim Bosnians could have theirs thrust upon them. What then, do Native Americans have to teach us about this process?

Native Americans

Like Italian Americans and Bosnian Muslims, Native Americans have reinvented themselves. There are, however, two important differences in this case. The first is the growth of a pan-Indian identity. It resembles the Italian instance only insofar as it is an identity originally imposed by outsiders and it replaces earlier identities connected with smaller units such as tribes or villages or reservations. It also parallels an increasing pan-Hispanic and pan-Asian movement in the contemporary United States. These peoples, who have accepted the larger definition of who they are, have, in fact, little else in common with each other than the stereotypes of the dominant group which labels them.

The second difference in the American Indian group may be unique. At least, I can think of no other ethnic group which has grown so rapidly from non-demographic sources:

Between 1960 and 1990, the number of Americans reporting American Indian as
their race in the U.S. Census more than tripled, growing from 523,591 to
1,878,285. This increase cannot be accounted for by the usual explanations of
population growth (e.g., increased births, decreased deaths).[17]

Nagel attributes this remarkable growth to what she calls "ethnic switching"—people identifying themselves as "Indian" who identified themselves
otherwise (probably 'white') in earlier census's. This Indian ethnic switching, like
the re-creation of Italian Americans and others, was in part an outgrowth of the
civil rights movement mentioned earlier. Carmichael's "black power" became
"red power" and the resulting Indian "movement of the 1960s and 1970s started
a tidal wave of ethnic renewal that surged across reservation and urban Indian
communities . . . encouraging individuals to claim and assert their 'Indianness.'"[18]

The peculiar thing observed by Nagel is not so much the shift in ethnicity—
an historically common phenomenon as it occurs in the assimilation process, but
the shift to *minority* ethnicity. The "playful" symbolic ethnicity, with its occa-
sional and hyphenated identity shifts, hardly qualifies. I am frankly uncertain how
religious conversion in the United States relates to all of this. Certainly the shift
from assimilated Jew to Orthodoxy is a choice of minority status. The shift from
Christian to Muslim among African Americans is understandable as an escape
from the religion of those who most recently enslaved their ancestors. The cost of
this shift is to embrace an additional minority status.

Although some fundamentalist Christians are converts, I suspect that they
tend to live in regions where most people are more or less like them. They would
be unlikely to think of themselves as minorities although other Americans might
perceive them as such. Although I have no data, I suspect that converts to
fundamentalist Muslim sects in the United States are rare. We did learn, following the attacks of September 2001, that some such communities do exist. These
issues, although important are not central to our discussion. Let us return to the
rather sudden appearance of large numbers of new Indians who are surely not
converts.

Who are all these new Indians? On the basis of census data and other
research evidence, Nagel is able to compare them to the total Indian population
and finds "these Indians are more urban, more concentrated in non-Indian states
without reservation communities, more often intermarried, less likely to assign
their mixed offspring an Indian race, and more likely to speak only English."[19]
Where did they come from? Nagel notes (1) the failure of many Indian veterans
and defense workers to return to reservations following World War II, (2) the
Eisenhower administration initiated urban relocation programs of the 1950s
which persisted into the 1970s, and of course, (3) the civil rights era with its
resurgence in ethnic pride.

There were also certain concrete benefits to being an Indian, such as land
claims awards, affirmative action, and minority set-aside programs. In fact, Nagel

writes, "Snipp reports concern among Native American educators about 'ethnic fraud' in the allocation of jobs and resources designated for American Indian students."[20] The influx of new Indians became so obvious that Indian tribal councils found it necessary to question who was and who was not eligible to call themselves Indian. Among the few peoples I am aware of who cling to the idea of racial purity so discredited by Ashley Montague were the German Nazis and the orthodox Jews. American Indians find themselves wrestling with this problem although they do not insist that they are either a super race or God's chosen people.

Conclusions

Where has this rambling essay on comparative ethnicity taken us? The volatility of the notions of race or ethnicity is such that, at least during this small moment in human history, the negative connotations and the negative consequences so clearly revealed in Ashley Montagu's work do not always exist. It is equally clear from recent events in Bosnia and Rwanda, that some of those evils do persist unrestrained. The three cases I have compared confirm Nagel's insistence that there is nothing primordial about ethnicity. She refers to "the growing literature documenting the shifting, volitional, situational nature of ethnicity" and devotes one of her articles to clarifying and organizing that literature.[21]

Both Nagel and Salmaone recognize the salience of the civil rights movement in a resurgent ethnic pride among Indians and Italian Americans. In failing to take note of this shift, Montague inevitably fails to take note of its consequences. There is increasing evidence that the renewed forms of American ethnicity are frequently symbolic—tied to such phenomena as folk art, festivals, costumes, historic myths, and food. The new immigrants, however, present a different picture. These Americans, mostly Asian and Hispanic, find themselves at the turn of this century repeating the patterns of intergroup relations typical of the turn of the last century.[22]

In the last chapter we saw evidence that people can call upon many identities, only one of which is ethnicity. Social class, gender, occupation, nationality, religion—these and others may become one's most prominent identity depending upon the social situation. The extent to which, under certain conditions, people arrange a permanent hierarchy of identities and the extent to which they shift situationally remains unclear.

Bosnian Muslims, American Indians, and Italian Americans all illustrate the process of ethnic renewal. The original ethnic identity of Indians and Italians was thrust upon them: they had no concept of themselves as Indians or Italians. It is the new Muslim identity which was thrust upon the Bosnians in place of their older Yugoslavian national identity. Note that the Bosnian Muslim shifts from a broad Yugoslav identity to a narrow ethnoreligious one. In contrast both the

American Indians and the Italian Americans shifted from original tribal or village identities to the much broader ones of Indian or Italian.

The shift from narrower to broader identities may be the better of the two. The Oliners,[23] in analyzing European rescuers of Jews during the Nazi era, developed the concept of "extensivity," which suggested that the broader the individual branches out to include larger groups within his or her notion of humanity, the more likely they are to identify with and come to the assistance of a persecuted minority. If we convert this psychological concept to a social one, it can be argued that, by extending minority definitions of themselves to larger and larger segments of the population, people will be less and less likely to persecute others. Following this logic even the silliness of inviting the whole world to join NATO makes sense. After all, if everyone belongs to the same army, who is there to have a war with? We hear more about the Oliners in chapter 9.

Montagu's work is not done.[24] He must brace himself for a seventh, eighth, ninth edition. Since the nineteenth century, the temptation to simplify and justify racial or ethnic differences on pseudo-scientific grounds has been too great to resist. My earliest recollection of this process actually is not directly related to race. It is the Italian physician Lombroso's demonstrations that head shape not only determined who was and who was not a criminal but also that precise analysis of the head would reveal the kinds of crimes one has a physical proclivity for. This sort of thing appears periodically: Hooton[25] (1946) on measurable physical characteristics, Sheldon[26] (1942) on body shape and temperament, Jensen[27] (1973) on intelligence and the brain, Herrnstein and Murray[27] (1994) on intelligence and IQ test scores.

Every twenty years or so there is a reprise of such "evidence" of racial superiority and inferiority much to the delight of the Nazis who still lurk in our midst. We need now to be wary of the popularity of genetics as an explanation for anything that offends some segment of society and to be particularly watchful of some of our colleagues who call themselves "socio-biologists." When I finished this last sentence, I heaved a sigh of relief and sat down with the morning paper. In the science section, I was faced with the headline, "Brain Scans Suggest Some Are Born with Violent Tendencies"—accompanied by three full color photos of illustrative brains.[28] It seems we have returned to Lombroso and to the last century. Could it be that these things are cyclical?

It is of course true that history takes its toll. If many immigrants (e.g., Irish, Italian, and Bosnian) have had ethnicity thrust upon them, it may be that in an era of mass communication and rapid transportation, authentic ethnic peoples may voluntarily retain an identity. This is the argument Laguerre proposes. He suggests that Japanese, Chinese, and Philippine immigrants to America retain close ties with and identify with their countries of origin. In fact he claims that one result of globalization is the reversal of whatever assimilation may have begun to occur among these groups.[29] In this first part of the book I have tried to spell out for the reader the nature of the problem of race and ethnicity, where it came from, and how it persists into the present. By now the reader may have noticed that my sources of data are sometimes unconventional. My academic background compels me to justify some of this. Let us finish part 1 with an explanation of where I found out what I know and why it isn't a bad place to look.

Notes

1. Thomas L Friedman., *The Lexus and the Olive Tree* (New York: Farrar, Straus Giroux, 1999), 27. For Friedman's parallel between the olive tree and the Lexus see 31-33.

2. Joane Nagel, "American Indian Ethnic Renewal: Politics and the Resurgence of Identity, *American Sociological Review* 60 (December 1995): 947.

3. Frank A Salmaone, "Deciding Who 'We' Are: The Order of the Sons of Italy and the Creation of Italian-American Ethnicity," *Journal of Human and Environmental Science* 1, no. 1 (spring 1996): 5, 16-17.

4. Frank A. Salmaone, "Deciding Who 'We' Are," 18.

5. Reginald Byron, *Irish America* (New York: Oxford University Press, 2000).

6. Frank A. Salmaone, "Deciding Who 'We' Are," 17.

7. Slavenka Drakulic, *Café Europa: Life After Communism* (New York: W. W. Norton, 1997).

8. Tone Bringa, *Being Muslim the Bosnia Way: Identity and Community in a Central Bosnian Village* (Princeton, N. J.: Princeton University Press, 1995), 8-9.

9. Bringa, *Being Muslim the Bosnian Way*, 224.

10. Bringa, *Being Muslim the Bosnian Way*, 202.

11. Bringa, *Being Muslim the Bosnian Way*, 204.

12. Bringa, *Being Muslim the Bosnian Way*, 3.

13. See Slavenka Drakulic, *Café Europa*, 210-11; Tone Bringa, *Being Muslim the Bosnian Way*, 3-4, 62, 149-51, 160, 204 (n 14); Blaine Hardin, "Some Say Bosnia Fight Not Ethnic," *Washington Post*, 14 June 1992, 25(A), 28(A); David B. Ottaway, "Weary Sarajevans Reaching for Multiethnic Normality," *Washington Post*, 24 December 1993, 10(A); Kemak Kurspahic, "The Saddest City," *Washington Post*, 9 February 1994, 23(A); Bogdan Denitch, "Now Bosnia without Bosnians," *Washington Post*, 13 February 1994, 1(C), 2(C).

14. Drakulic, *Café Europa*, 210-11.

15. Bringa, *Being Muslim the Bosnian Way*, 36.

16. Drakulic, *Café Europa*, 210.

17. Nagel, "American Indian," 947.

18. Nagel, "American Indian," 948.

19. Nagel, "American Indian," 953.

20. Joane Nagel, "Constructing Ethnicity: Creating and Recreating Ethnic Identity and Culture," *Social Problems* 41 (February 1994): 160. Her reference is to C. Mathew Snipp, "Some Observations about Racial Boundaries and the Experiences of American Indians." (paper presented at the University of Washington, Seattle Washington, April 1993).

21. Nagel, "Constructing Ethnicity," 153.

22. As mentioned in chapter 4, Fletcher's report on Compton, California, describes a Los Angeles area reminiscent of New York City a century ago: an immigrant press,

struggles with older immigrants for control of public jobs, interethnic battles over turf and control of local businesses, exclusive ethnic communities (ghettos), and the whole array of vicious stereotypes fostered by the larger white society. See Michael A. Fletcher, "The Myth of the Melting Pot: America's Racial and Ethnic Divides," *Washington Post,* 7 April 1998, 1(A) and 4-5(A).

23. Samuel Oliner and Pearl M. Oliner, *The Altruistic Personality: Rescuers of Jews in Nazi Europe* (New York: The Free Press, 1988).

24. Ashley Montagu, *Man's Most Dangerous Myth: The Fallacy of Race*, 6th ed., abridged student edition (Walnut Creek, Calif.: Alta Mira Press, 1997).

25. E. A. Hooton, *Up from the Ape* (New York: Macmillan, 1946).

26. W. H. Sheldon with the collaboration of S.S. Stevens, *The Varieties of Temperament* (New York: Harper & Brothers, 1942).

27. Arthur Jensen, *Educability and Group Difference* (New York: Harper and Row, 1973).

28. Richard J. Herrnstein and Charles Murray, *The Bell Curve: Intelligence and Class Structure in American Life* (New York: The Free Press, 1994).

29. Rob Stein, "Brain Scans Suggest Some Are Born with Violent Tendencies," *Washington Post,* 13 April 1998, 3(A).

30. Michael S. Laguerre, *The Global Ethnopolis: Chinatown, Japantown, and Manilatown in American Society* (New York: St. Martin's Press, 1999).

Chapter 6

Reporters for the Daily Press: A Worldwide Network of Research Assistants

A recent book on U.S. Indian policy . . . written by a historian, consigns to the "Secondary Works" section of the bibliography the results of Margaret Mead's pioneering original field study of a contemporary reservation culture . . .. I first ran into this bit of historian superciliousness in a book on the Ojibwa that bibliographically listed Ruth Landes's classic ethnographic works as "secondary sources" in contradistinction to the "primary" documentary sources (no matter how superficial and transitory might have been the event that prompted the document).

— J. Anthony Paredes, "SFAA President's Letter." *Society for Applied Anthropology Newsletter* 4, no. 4 (November 1993): 1-2

Historians like it straight from the horse's mouth no matter how high the horse. They do have their own peculiar definitions of what constitute secondary sources, but they are not alone. Let me provide what is possibly a primary source for my statement. In his review of the first draft of a recent book, an editor said to me,"You have admitted to using secondary sources." I was indignant since I had no intention of admitting anything. I had simply acknowledged my sources as any scholar is expected to do. What I had acknowledged was an interpretation of Hegel provided by a distinguished historian of social philosophy. Apparently the editor was of the opinion that I should have gone directly to Hegel and provided my own interpretation. I didn't agree then and don't agree now. Did you ever try to read Hegel? But that editor aroused my curiosity about the concept of secondary sources.

This is an issue particularly relevant to this book since it is heavily dependent upon newspaper reports. I view such reports as anecdotal or as case studies, to use the more acceptable social science synonym. In some earlier writing, I had made an effort to synthesize many years of research on Project Head Start.[1] At that time, I treated single pieces of research as "anecdotes"—short informative accounts of something that happened. Although some are more informative than others, every piece of research standing on its own remains no more than an anecdote.[2] It is only when such anecdotal evidence begins to converge in a single direction that we can have confidence in its credibility. In this sense, scientific evidence is a set of anecdotes. In this chapter I argue that newspaper accounts are of the same genre: Standing by itself any one article, like any one experiment or ethnography, is anecdotal. It is the independent reproduction of such anecdotes which turns them into credible evidence.

The columnist Dave Barry, writing in a sarcastic vein (I hope), makes precisely the opposite argument of that made in this chapter:

> In the newspaper business (motto: "Trust us! We're English Majors!"), we have high standards of accuracy. Before we print anything we make sure that:
> *We personally believe it's true, or
> *A reliable source (defined as "a source wearing business attire") told us it's true, or
> *Another newspaper, with a respectable newspaper name such as "The Fort Smidling Chronic Truncator" says it's true, or
> *It's getting late and we need to print SOMETHING so we can go to the bar.[3]

Barry's point about "The Fort Smidling Chronic Truncator" becomes a serious issue later in this chapter. For the moment, it is important to recognize that I found his column in the New York tabloid, the *Daily News*. My newspaper sources are by and large from the *Washington Post*. One of its most distinguished and senior editors writes that when she left Greenwich Village and came to work at the *Post*, she discovered a new kind of reporting. Meg Greenfield describes a process of "transforming" from an opinionated liberal into a detached professional journalist. Her objective shifted from "being right in one's own estimation and that of like-minded friends to getting it right."[4] She observes that what she discovered in the process was often not in conformity with her previously held and preferred interpretation.

A tabulation of references in this book up to this point reveals that all of those in chapter 1 are scholarly citations. But chapter 2 is a different story. Of the fifty references cited there, thirty-six (72 percent) are from newspapers and magazines —mostly the *Washington Post,* which is my hometown newspaper. In chapter 3 about two-thirds of the references are to academic sources. The extent to which I use newspaper reports varies depending on the subject of the chapter. The point is that I use newspaper reports a lot and most of the ones I use are from the *Washington Post*. The question is: "How good is newspaper reporting compared to academic reporting?" Is there, as Barry hints and Greenfield would deny, something tainted about my journalistic sources?

What, precisely, do we mean when we refer to secondary sources? The large data banks from which flow much contemporary sociological research are surely secondary sources. Those who employ such data have little notion of how valid or reliable the process leading to their publication may be. Julius Roth[5] has documented the manner in which underpaid, poorly trained, part-time pollsters serve as the hired hands who gather such stuff. French survey researchers were observed to behave in the same manner a couple of decades later.[6] In fact Hanson argues convincingly that there are both theoretical bases and empirical evidence that social scientists rigorously train raters to achieve uniform ratings which have nothing to do with objective features of the material being rated.[7]

Presumably a primary source would be a report received directly from an observer of an event. Eyewitness reports, however, are held to be notoriously unreliable by both lawyers and social scientists. In any event, unless the analyst was the eyewitness, these reports are also secondary in that they are filtered through an observer to the analyst. According to this devious line of reasoning, the historians are correct in relegating Margaret Mead and Ruth Landes to their secondary source bibliographies. Ethnographic field workers, who are in my estimate the epitome of primary data gatherers, frequently rely on informants.

Elizabeth Loftus, a University of Washington psychologist who serves as an expert witness, reminds us that "The mind is a mischievous trickster that blends facts with fancy. Not only does the original picture fade, but it actually changes with new bits of information."[8] Her primary example is the possibility that ten different witnesses may have misidentified John Demjanjuk as Ivan the Terrible, a Nazi death camp guard. Although juries find eyewitness accounts highly convincing, experts like Loftus contend mistakes are distressingly common and a major cause of wrongful convictions. On July 28, 1993, the Israeli supreme court reversed the conviction of Demjanjuk and ordered him released.

Think about your own biography for a moment! What happened when and are you sure? Throughout the year 2000 a reputable Korean War veteran insisted that he had machine gunned innocent civilians under a bridge during a retreat early in that war (1950). He truly believed he had, but careful newspaper reporters discovered that he had not been at that place at that time and he later confessed that he must have confused things he had heard and told with reality.[9] When a friend of mine argued that I had been wounded during the Second World War and should rightly have received a purple heart, the Marine Corps pointed out that a wound merited that medal only if received in combat. Of the three times my airplane fell into the Pacific Ocean only one was due to enemy fire. Sixty years later I could not honestly argue that it was the one which caused my injury. At the time, the important thing was to get out of the airplane safely, not why the airplane fell down.

It is difficult to imagine data sources which are not secondary. Like ethnographers, but more plentiful and more public with their data, newspaper reporters at the site of events may provide data as primary as can be found. One social scientist who depended heavily upon local newspaper archives for her data concludes that the local newspaper's major bias is not so much deliberate distortion of facts but rather ignoring or neglecting certain events.[10] The other side of this coin is that a free press can, although it may not, correct for class-biased omissions. Writing of Brazilian history, Andrews observes that: "While members of the Black middle class have left abundant evidence of their individual and collective concerns, slaves and workers, most of them illiterate, have left little or no documentary record of their lives and times."[11] The press can provide a corrective for a class bias that probably exists in all societies where the literate (and presumably the controlling) classes record history from their own perspective, while the illiterate can find their point of view expressed only in whatever sympathetic press may exist—unless, of course, there happens to be an anthropologist on the scene. One would wish there had been one present among Native Americans during the period 1820-1890. Coward reports on the universal stereotypes perpetrated by the press during that period.[12]

Like scientists, contemporary newspaper reporters are trained to exercise a degree of detachment, value objectivity, check the reliability of their sources, and confirm their discoveries with outside evidence. Both scientists and journalists are subject to scrutiny by their peers and to both internal and external sanctions should their integrity be questioned. In a real sense the careers of both are contingent upon their maintenance of credibility. Reporters who engage in such misconduct as fabrication, falsification, or plagiarism endanger not only their own careers but the reputations of their newspapers as well. This is as true of scientists as it is of journalists (not just social scientists, but all kinds of scientists).

I want to suggest that, to the extent that there is external social constraint combined with an internalized ethic, there is assurance of the reliability of the data source. This is a matter of degree: there is always more or less social constraint and more or less of an internalized ethic. Lest we consider scientists above such sordid behavior as "fabrication, falsification, or plagiarism," consider a report issued on April 22, 1992, by a panel of American scientists and engineers.[13] They tell us that the problem of scientific fraud has become so severe that traditional self-correcting mechanisms within science are no longer sufficient to cope with it.

I mention this report, not because I wish to discredit scientific evidence, but for two other reasons: (1) it suggests that scientific evidence is probably no more or less credible than evidence derived from other professional sources with similar controls placed on them, and (2) what I have said so far about the report is based, not on the report itself, but on an article in the *Washington Post*.[14] This is secondary data. I will use it below as an example of how I think we need to deal with press reports.

The chairman of that scientific panel told the reporter that "what we are saying is that there is a real problem and it's serious." The vocabulary I employed above to describe misconduct among reporters is borrowed from the panel's definition of scientific misconduct: "Fabrication, falsification, or plagiarism in proposing, performing, or reporting research." The data which is the cause of such great alarm is also reported in the *Post* article. We find that the concern is based largely on over 200 allegations of scientific misconduct reported to federal agencies during 1989 and 1990. Thirty of these were confirmed.

As difficult as it may be to judge the credibility of these figures, it seems that when one considers the tens of thousands of scientists engaged in their craft during that time, the data seem insufficient to justify either the panel chairman's or the reporter's insistence that there is a severe problem of scientific fraud. There may well be, but these data do not support such a claim. What I have just done is to discount the evidence. But is it the evidence of the report or the evidence of the reporter that I am discounting? I will return to this question in a moment. To this point, everything I have said about scientific cheating comes from the newspaper reporter. The concept of discounting evidence is central to all analysis but there is an important distinction which must be made between two types of newspaper reports.

Facts versus Interpretation

There are two kinds of information available from newspaper articles. One is what may be described as "factual" (in spite of the postmodernists claim that there are no facts but only interpretations). Examples of facts would include the number of Russians living in former Soviet republics other than Russia or the numbers and names of major ethnic groups, languages, alphabets, and religions found in the former Yugoslavia. Like the U.S. census these may not be entirely accurate,[15] but they provide the best estimate available.

One could uncover such facts in the library, but why is that method superior to permitting a journalist to do the research? Is the journalist less responsible than the graduate assistant who would dig up the data for us? At their best, newspeople meet all of the standards applied by the scholar. One reporter mentions "the cable found in the National Archives" and then describes his procedures: "Research in seven presidential libraries and the National Archives and interviews with dozens of former officials provided new information about a 50-year U.S. involvement in the region." In an endnote the *Post* staff writer describes this as "a three month project."[16]

The use of factual information gleaned from the newspaper seems to me an economical way to grasp facts from a great many parts of the world without having to become an area specialist in all of them. It saves not only time and effort, but permits much broader comparative research than would otherwise be possible. Furthermore, the facts reported by the press are likely to be more up-to-date than any easily available published source. It is of particular interest to the applied social scientist that this process is much faster and cheaper than the alternatives. Imagine the formidable travel budget, the decades of tracking down information and interpreting it properly, the acquisition of at least a rudimentary familiarity with dozens of languages, and ultimately organizing and analyzing the warehouses full of information collected. It would be decades before such a project would see the light of publication.

The objective of this book is to delineate national policies which deal successfully with intergroup relations. We will get to that in part 2. To pursue this objective it is necessary to identify types of conditions which give rise to types of relations and this in turn requires the comparison of national cases. The linguist Christina Paulston argues correctly that "The comparison of case studies is probably the most fruitful approach to the study of language and ethnicity." She views this as the means for searching out causal factors and identifying the types of social conditions related to them.[17]

The second kind of information available from the press involves "interpretation" of the facts. It is likely that most reporting of events entails interpretation, whether deliberate or not. It is the responsibility of the analyst employing such data to read it critically—to discount it appropriately. It should be clear that this same process is required of the analyst when examining tomes produced by scholars in international relations, economics, political science, sociology, anthropology, or whatever. A responsible scholar does not accept the evidence at face value, no matter what its source. All research, scientific and journalistic, is flawed. The question is a matter of extent or degree.

Although I treat "facts" and "interpretation" as if they were two distinct categories, the distinction may often be blurred. The examples found in this chapter come from the extremes of a continuum ranging from most factual to most interpretive. Nevertheless, I find the distinction to be a useful methodological device and will continue to employ it as if it was a dichotomy. Another problem which I have chosen to ignore in this discussion is the selective judgment which enters into the definition of what constitutes "news"—on the part of both reporters and editors. The distortion introduced here is one of omission. This is closely related to Jill Stephen's observations of bias in the local press.[18] There is information which is simply unavailable through the press. The role of newspaper editors in this gatekeeping process has been thoroughly documented.[19] With these caveats in mind, let us consider the process which C. Wright Mills described as "discounting."[20]

Discounting the Evidence

Discounting is essentially a matter of independent confirmation by (1) comparison with the original source; (2) internal comparison by the analyst with his or her extant body of knowledge and judgment; or (3) comparison with independent sources. The description of the science panel report mentioned earlier consists of some data excerpted by the reporter and a few quotes from the chairman. On this limited basis, it seemed to me that the reporter and the panel chairman were overstating the seriousness of the issue (comparison 2).

Because there is probably more data presented in the report itself and because those data might be subject to different interpretations than those posed by the reporter and the chairman, or might confirm their alarm, the analyst cannot rely solely on the newspaper article. This is especially true when the original report is easily available. Checking the original report (comparison 1), I find that the data presented are correct even though incomplete but that it is my interpretation rather than the panel chairman's which is confirmed in the report itself. It refers to the "infrequent incidents of misconduct in science" and notes, as I did above, that "When measured against the denominator of the number of research awards or research investigators, the range of misconduct-in-science cases cited above is small." The report elaborates on and documents that observation.[21]

Finally, a comparison with independent sources became available (comparison 3) in November 1993 with the release of a national study of misconduct in science prepared by Swazey and colleagues at the Acadia Institute in Maine. According to the *New York Times*, that study "showed that 43 percent of students and 50 percent of faculty members reported direct knowledge of more than one kind of [scientific] misconduct in their labs."[22] The alarm of the original panel study appears to have been justified, in spite of my doubts.

A more general, and perhaps obvious example, of the requirement to check original sources when appropriate is provided by book reviews. I was tempted to use as a source, a review by Etzioni of Schlesinger's *The Disuniting of America*.[23] Having read Schlesinger, I am grateful that I did not succumb to the temptation. Even so reliable and reputable a scholar as Etzioni cannot do justice to such an impassioned and informed essay dealing directly with my central research concerns.

The second kind of discounting derived, in my case, from my background in sociology occurs when it is either impossible or unnecessary to check original sources. For example, Blaine Harden, a *Post* writer who provided informed on-the-spot reports from Eastern Europe for many years, examines the revival of anti-Semitism in that part of the world. His column, datelined Sofia, reviews the refusal of the Bulgarians to cooperate with the Nazis in deporting Jews and otherwise documents a history of tolerance and cooperation between Bulgarian Jews and their hosts.[24]

It may be, as the elderly president of the Bulgarian Jewish Council claims, that "Jews are respected and credible to non-Jews." But elsewhere in the article we learn that between 1948 and 1953 about 45,000 of the then 50,000 Jews in Bulgaria migrated to Israel "with the help of the Bulgarian government." Only 5,000 chose to remain and, in 1990, there were about 3,500 Jews in Bulgaria. In that year 800 young Bulgarian Jews were planning to leave for Israel. It is possible that the pressure stems from attraction to Israel rather than from repulsion for Bulgaria. Nevertheless, when over 90 percent of Bulgarian Jews have fled the country leaving a residue of a few thousand mostly elderly people, the comment by one of them raises questions of credibility for me: "As far as I know from my life," says the informant, "everybody in my country likes Jews." It appears that it is not prudent to buy everything in this largely informative column; some discounting is necessary.

A different example of discounting based on sociological background is found in the analysis of the Korean community in the Washington, D.C., area.

Joel Garreau, a *Post* staff writer, finds it odd that, unlike the enclaves of nineteenth-century immigrants, Washington has no Koreatown. Garreau writes: "The main reason is the overwhelming value Koreans place on education for their children, according to real estate agents and sociologists."[25] His informants do indeed insist that, when looking for housing, their prime criteria are price, neighborhood, and schools. But that is not peculiarly Korean. There are good public schools in Washington's plushier neighborhoods, but the reason most people with young families go to the suburbs is, at least in part, related to the affordability of housing.

Housing of adequate size for a young, expanding, middle-class family is much more expensive in the city than in the suburbs. There is a fear about security in the city and (as witnessed in the Los Angeles riots of 1992) Koreans can be expected to share the same racism as other Americans. In addition to these suggestions of the implausibility of the education explanation, Garreau's sample is exclusively middle-class, professional, college educated. Not a single Korean street vender or shopkeeper, so visible in Washington, is to be found among them. This sort of quick and dirty critique of an otherwise informative article is necessary if it is to be properly discounted and used intelligently as I try to do in chapter 13.

The third discounting procedure, independent confirmation, may sometimes be possible and certainly ought to be sought. Thus, when I read of an enormously successful piece of legislation in Ghana called the Chieftaincy Act, I was both impressed and suspicious. It claimed that, among other things, a long history of tribal animosity and brutal warfare had been ended in Ghana by the central government simply by granting tribes complete control over tribal matters within tribal territory while the central government reserved the right to manage international relations, wars with foreign powers, national taxation, and other fiscal and monetary matters. The act required local chiefs to meet regularly and consider whatever problems they might have with boundaries and the like. This appears to be the sort of thing that might work in Afghanistan or might have worked in Bosnia had it been implemented in time. After reading this in the *Washington Post*, I sought and obtained confirmation of its success from two Ghanaian graduate students in America, one exiled politician in England, and both a visiting scholar and a cab driver in Washington. The Ghanaian solution is further considered in chapter 8.

Conclusion

There may be a literature on the proper use of the press as a source of data. If so I am not familiar with it. I am familiar with Robert E. Park's definition of the sociologist as "a kind of super reporter" in search of the "Big News"[26] This notion of Park's was introduced in chapter 2. He and his colleagues viewed the immigrant press as an important source of data as well as an object of study.

Perhaps the first enduring piece of sociological literature to emerge from the Chicago School which Park founded was Thomas and Znaniecki's 1927 publication, *The Polish Peasant in Europe and America*.[27] The data on which those volumes are based consists largely of diaries, letters, journals, and reports in the press—both Polish and Polish American. It is my understanding that the historian would allow the first three as "primary" but not the press reports.

Park's "super reporters" do in fact exist and they do search for what he called the "big news." Thomas Friedman is the foreign affairs columnist for the *New York Times*. His description of his work seems to paraphrase Park's description of the sociologist:

> I can go anywhere anytime and have attitudes about what I see and hear. But the question for me as I embarked on this odyssey was: which attitudes? What would be the lens, the perspective, the organizing system—the superstory through which I would look at the world, make sense of events, prioritize them, opine upon them and help readers understand them?[28]

Friedman is not alone among journalists who resemble sociologists in Park's sense. With the help of economists working with the IMF and the World Bank, Steven Mufson reports that "Cures for a nation's financial ills are similar, whether for Russia, Bolivia or Ghana."[29] Glenn Frankel titles a series of three articles on Northern Ireland, Israel, and South Africa, "Triangle of Intolerance" and begins with the observation that these three instances of dominant-minority conflict must share some things in common.[30] Unfortunately, he treats each of his three stories in isolation from the other two.

A final caveat concerns the variety of the press. Judgment must be exercised in estimating the extent to which a source is responsible and ethical. The *Washington Post* or the *New York Times* or the *Christian Science Monitor*, and their staffs, are to be granted more credibility than the *National Enquirer* and other tabloids to be found at the supermarket checkout counter. The Sunday July 25, 1993, comic strip *Outland*, depicting three animals peering into their underwear, was refused publication by the *Houston Post* because of the possibility that it might offend some of its readers. It makes you wonder what else—including news—they choose to omit out of fear of offending some readers. Clearly not all American newspapers are equally open in their concepts of what constitutes news. Local knowledge is needed in judging most local newspapers. Some conform to the highest journalistic standards; others to the lowest. This is, unfortunately, also true of universities.

In America, it is generally assumed that Harvard or Stanford and similar reputable institutions hold their faculties to the highest standards. But there is also Brigham Young University, whose archaeologists provide documentation that it was not ancient astronauts but, rather Jesus himself who flew into pre-Columbian South and Central America and whose image is found in the decaying sculptures of those civilizations. Elsewhere in the United States one can find fundamentalist Christian universities with departments of "Creationism," an utterly implausible bit of mysticism. Universities, along with the press, must suffer the likes of the *National Enquirer*. All universities, like all newspapers, are not equal.

I have at my disposal, for the price of a daily newspaper, hundreds of well-trained research assistants—observing, interviewing, bringing to bear their familiarity and experience in the exotic corners of the world, and writing regular and timely reports for me. If sometimes they are selective in what they do and do not tell me; if sometimes their sampling could be improved; if sometimes their informants lack plausibility; if sometimes I have information which suggests that they are incorrect; then I must guard against these problems. My research assistants employed by the world press do very well by me.

My discussion is not really concerned with the question of what is and is not a secondary source. Historians are free to categorize evidence as they please. My concern is with the misleading semantics. The very term secondary suggests inferiority and is often prefaced with such descriptors as "mere" or "only." It may be that at times secondary sources can be shown to be inferior to primary ones. At other times, it is clear that secondary sources are the superior ones. That is, of course, Paredes's point in the quotation that opened this chapter. The quotation which opens chapter 8 makes it clear that there was little in the way of relevant professional literature available in the 1980s when I embarked upon this work. Without the help of the press, the work would not have been possible.

Much of what has been discussed in this chapter might fall under the more dignified title, "methodology." It is partly a defense of the logic of my procedure. The issues and logic have been set forth. Enough of background and preliminaries! Let us turn to what if anything can be done to put an end to the painful manner in which most nations mistreat their minorities. We shall see that some do not treat them badly at all and the result is a happy one for both the nation and its peoples.

Notes

1. Irwin Deutscher, "Project Head Start and the Cognitive Police," in *Making A Difference: The Practice of Sociology* (New Brunswick, N.J.: Transaction Publishers, 1999).

2. I have taken the liberty of substituting "informative" for *Webster's Unabridged*, "entertaining." This modern usage also can eliminate the word "short" from *Webster's* definition. *Webster's* synonyms include "story," "incident," "tale," and "narrative," all suitable for present purposes.

3. Dave Barry, "She Has Bone to Pick about Talkin' Turkey," *Daily News*, 20 January 2001, 18.

4. Meg Greenfield, *Washington Public Affairs*, Washington, D.C., 2001.

5. Julius Roth, "Hired Hand Research." *American Sociologist* 1, no.1 (November 1965): 190-96.

6. Jean Peneff, "The Observers Observed: French Survey Researchers at Work," *Social Problems* 35, no. 5 (December 1988): 520-34.

7. Barbara Gail Hanson, "Human Rulers: The Constructivist Question in Reliability

Based on Inter-Rater Agreement," *Methodology and Science* (1993): 1-4.

8. References to Elizabeth Loftus are from an interview by LaFraniere, "Identifying 'Ivan': Does Memory Mislead?" *Washington Post*, 27 August 1992, 25(A).

9. The reporter Michael Dobbs provides an example of methodology and historiography in his focus on the reliablity of both eyewitnesses and documentary evidence in his research on this matter. See his, "Truth and Other Casualties of *No Gun Ri*," *Washington Post*, 21 May 2000, 1(B) and 5(B).

10. Jill D. Stevens, "Reconstructing Reality: Using News Articles as Data" (paper read at the annual meetings of the North Central Sociological Association, Toledo, Ohio, 17 April 1993).

11. I discovered this insightful quote in a review of Andrews' book by Neckerman. The exact same point is made by Sheldon in his history of criminal justice. He reminds us that history is constructed from the documents and perspectives of the wealthy, suggesting that the real threat to life and property comes from such sources as the "dangerous classes." Sheldon insists that it is the offenses of the wealthy which have caused the greatest harm. See George Reid Andrews, *Blacks and Whites in Sao Paulo, Brazil, 1888-1988* (Madison: University of Wisconsin Press, 1991); Kathryn M. Neckerman, "Review of Andrews', *Blacks and Whites in Sao Paulo, Brazil, 1888-1988*," *Contemporary Sociology* 22, no. 2: (March 1993): 179-80; Randall G. Sheldon, *Controlling the Dangerous Classes: A Critical Introduction to the History of Criminal Justice* (Boston: Allyn and Bacon, 2001).

12. John M. Coward, *The Newspaper Indian: Native American Identity in the Press, 1820-90* (Urbana: University of Illinois Press, 1999).

13. Panel on Scientific Responsibility and the Conduct of Research, *Responsible Science: Ensuring the Integrity of the Research Process*, Vol. I (Washington, D.C.: National Academy Press, 1992).

14. Boyce Rensberger, "Science Panel Cites Research Fraud Problem," *Washington Post*, 23 April 1992, 11(A).

15. The racial and ethnic categories provided by the 1990 U.S. Census failed to satisfy some 200,000 Americans who preferred to identify themselves by such categories as "child of God," "California boy," "Heinz 57," "brown," "A fine blend," "None of your business," or (a category provided by the census) "other." But never fear, "The computer was able to assign about 85 percent of these 'unique responses.'" So much for facts! My source is not the Census Bureau but a report in the *Dayton Daily News*, 12 May 1991, 19(A). The press enjoyed reporting a replay of this scenario a decade later, even though the census had considerably expanded the choices it had provided a decade earlier.

16. Walter Pincus, "Secret Presidential Pledges," *Washington Post*, 9 February 1992, 20(A).

17. Christina Bratt Paulston, "International Perspectives on Multilingualism and Language Policies" (paper read at Conference on Language and Ethnicity, Baku, Azerbaijan, June 1988).

18. Jill D. Stevens, "Reconstructing Reality," 1993.

19. The pioneering piece of work on editorial gatekeeping is David M. White, "The 'Gatekeeper,'A Case Study in the Selection of News," *Journalism Quarterly* 28 (1950): 283-90.

20. C.Wright Mills, "Methodological Consequences of the Sociology of Knowledge," *American Journal of Sociology* 46 (1940): 316-30.

21. Panel on Scientific Responsibility, *Responsible Science*, 80 and 96 n.2.

22. Philip J. Hilts, "Pure Science? Not Always," *New York Times*, November 1993. The original study is Judith Swazey et al., "Scientific Misconduct Survey," *American Scientist* (October 1993).

23. Amitai Etzioni, "The Perils of American Tribalism" (Review of Schlesinger, 1991), *Washington Post*, "Book World," 8 September 1992, 4. The book is Arthur M. Schlesinger Jr., *The Disuniting of America: Reflections on a Multicultural Society* (New York: W. W. Norton, 1991).

24. Blaine Hardin, "Bulgaria and Its Jews," *Washington Post*, 31 December 1990, 10(A).

25. Joel Garreau, "Area Koreans See No Need for Enclaves," *Washington Post*, 11 January 1992, 1(E) and 8-9(E).

26. Robert E. Park, *The Immigrant Press and Its Control* (New York: Harper & Brothers, 1922). I am most grateful to Stanford M. Lyman for the pains he took to locate and inform me of this citation as well as other useful materials. I had previously mistakenly referred to Park's "The Big Story." Easy access to Park's work is provided by Everett C. Hughes *et al.* (eds.), *Race and Culture: The Collected Papers of Robert Ezra Park*, Vol.1 (Glencoe, Ill.: Free Press, 1950).

27. W. I. Thomas, and Florian Znaniecki, *The Polish Peasant in Europe and America* (New York: Knopf, 1927).

28. Thomas L. Friedman, *The Lexus and the Olive Tree* (New York: Farrar, Straus & Giroux, 1999). 5.

29. Steven Mufson, "Shock Therapy for Sick Economies," *Washington Post*, 5 January 1992, 1(H).

30. Glenn Frankel, "Triangle of Intolerance," *Washington Post*, 19 January 1992.

Part 2

**Toward Solutions: From Time to Time and
Place to Place**

Chapter 7

Backdrop and Precursors

The horrifying examples of human and material disaster in recent year—in Rwanda, the former Yugoslavia and East Timor—tell us much about our failure to take preventive measures to avoid violent conflicts.

— Anna Lindh, Swedish foreign minister in an editorial, "Create a Worldwide Culture of Conflict Prevention," *International Herald Tribune,* 18-19 September 1999.

The Swedish foreign minister makes the point that the act of prevention is universal. She reminds us that we routinely take measures to prevent crop destruction and to protect livestock from predators. All sorts of preventive measures are taken to avoid air, rail, and highway accidents. "Insurance policies," writes Lindh, "are developed in almost all areas of human activity." Why then, she wonders, do we not act to prevent the kinds of human disasters this book deals with?

It is true that we have often failed to take preventive measures even though such measures may be readily available. In part 1, I made an effort to lay the groundwork for what is to follow. To be sure the kinds of policies discussed here are unlikely to *eliminate* intergroup violence, but I do believe that they can

Note: The chapters in part 2 are an expanded and updated version of "From Time to Time and Place to Place: Ethnic Policies That Work" (paper presented at an international conference, Global to Local Governance: Policy Development, organized by Research Committee 26 of the International Sociological Association, Chania [Crete], Greece, 28-31 May 1997).

reduce it considerably. I am pessimistic enough, however, to suppose that members of human groups will persist in hurting and killing members of other human groups who they define as different from themselves.

Although pessimistic, I am not as fatalistic and resigned as Shils, or Orlans who cites (and presumably agrees with) him. Shils insists that there is no permanent solution to any important problem in human life and further he states: "It does not lie within the powers possessed by human beings to do much about [this]."[1] Ronald Cohen neatly sums up this Hobbsian world view:

> There is a widespread assumption that these [ethnic and racial] conflicts are atavistic outcroppings from less enlightened times. . . . Increased tensions, fundamentalism, and ethnocentrism are simply reactionary downward blips on the upward curve to a more tolerant and more decent tomorrow. Possibly. But in no way demonstrated by science or by the events of the past few years.[2]

There are two counter positions to the gloomy Orlans-Shils philosophy. One is the relativistic stance taken by Reece McGee. Like Cohen, he suspects that things have been worse and may be getting better. He believes that an objective appraisal of world history of the past two millennia,

> *does* demonstrate some degree of what could reasonably be called "moral progress" for the race as a whole. A great deal of frightfulness which would have been taken for granted a thousand years ago is widely condemned today. Few people are burned at the stake by official action anymore, nor is anyone nailed to a cross. Torture is fairly widely abhorred and not too many get stoned as witches. Mass murder is widely condemned and nowhere nearly as widely practiced as it used to be. And when it happens it sometimes gets punished, or at least stopped. These are real net gains in morality of behavior.[3]

The other more optimistic view is the one which is reflected in part 2. It is less evolutionary and more action-oriented: there are policies which constrain collective meanness. They work only under clearly specified conditions and only from time to time and from place to place. A few of them are identified in part 2. There is no need to study history in order to discover the mistreatment an ethnic group can impose on its neighbors. In the last decade of the millennium we witnessed not only such dramatic instances as those mentioned by Lindh in the opening of this chapter but also the less publicized massacres perpetrated by Mexican soldiers on Mayan villagers and the vicious attacks on Chinese and their property everywhere in Indonesia. Is there no end to it? Given enough time even the most persistent and seemingly hopeless of conflicts such as those between Protestants and Catholics in Northern Ireland and between Palestinians and Israelis in the Middle East show faint glimmers of hope. But from time to time we find more than faint glimmers.

There are sometimes peoples who manage not to hurt one another. This is the positive if less dramatic story I have to tell. In all of the gloom there are bits of light.[4] I am certainly not the first to make positive suggestions for the solution of interethnic problems. In earlier editions of his work, Ashley Montagu urged educational programs as a solution to the ignorance which prevailed. Although his faith in this particular policy has been shaken, he does provide references to several articles suggesting peaceful coexistence between ethnic groups.[5] Montagu led me to an anthropological literature dating just prior to the Second World War. Robert Redfield while studying Guatemalan Indians, was stimulated to make some comparative observations.[6] The stimulus was a report by Lindgren of relations between Reindeer-Tungas and Russian Cossacks of northwestern Manchuria.[7] Redfield writes that the generally cordial relations he observed between the culturally Spanish Ladinos and the culturally Mayan Indios, closely parallels the relations observed in Manchuria. The anthropologists both describe these as relationships without conflict. In both cases no expressions of fear, hatred, or contempt are heard and there have been no instances reported of the use or threat of force.

What are the conditions which appear to give rise to this "benign character of intergroup relations"? The key seems to be the individualistic character of social and economic relations. The individual and the immediate household or family are the responsible units. There are no clans or extended community responsibilities. As Redfield sums it up, in both cases, "what a man does has small consequences for larger groups and little for his ethnic group. The success of an Indian does not 'raise his race' any more than a delict by an Indian brings shame upon Indians as such." Beyond this there have been no recent attempts by one group to dominate the other, natural resources are plentiful, and both groups make their living in the same manner. Finally, it is important to note that neither Spaniards nor Cossacks brought with them strong traditions of prejudice based on skin color or physical type.

In a study of another Guatemalan community, shortly after Redfield's work, John Gillin selects as the subject of his article "the contact between 'races' without conflict."[8] Gillin accounts for the lack of conflict with the fact that the Indian group does not feel excessively frustrated. "How," he asks, "is this to be explained?" Gillin points out that the Indians have developed a satisfying culture of their own and that they are actually and theoretically free. When things go wrong, he finds, Indians blame either themselves or the distant "government." They do not find fault with their neighbor Ladinos who are by and large as impoverished as they. There exist side by side two distinct cultures which are not always mutually understood but which are always tolerated.

From these observations of people's who coexist without conflict, we learn that such interethnic relations are possible and we learn something of the conditions which nurture them. There is another related strain in the literature, this one more contemporary. The field of conflict resolution has evolved from at least three sources: labor-management negotiations, international diplomacy, and efforts to help people resolve interpersonal problems without violence. Conflict resolution is an interdisciplinary undertaking which focuses on what its practitioners call "problem solving." The process includes an array of techniques designed to fit different kinds of conflict situations at different stages: workshops, negotiations, mediation, crisis management. Kriesberg, for example, identifies successful cases of mediation (1991, 1996). These and similar clinical processes are designed to work at both the interpersonal and the intergroup level.[9]

The orientation of part 2 is different from both anthropological observations and conflict resolution in that it seeks to discover instances in which nation-states have developed and implemented policies which prevent or control ethnic conflict. Although there may be difference in our orientation, there is no difference in our objectives. Kriesberg insists that "Noting successes, not just failures, may embolden a variety of actors to attempt early preventive actions." Mirroring with precision my own concerns, Kriesberg reminds us:

> Relatively little attention is given to relationships that are peaceful or nonviolently contentious. Attention, however, should be given to such cases so that we might learn what prevented them from becoming bloody and protracted struggles, and so that they might serve as models for what human beings can and do achieve.[10]

Arthur M. Schlesinger, Jr. believes that the noun "ethnicity" had its modest beginning in 1940 in W. Lloyd Warner's Yankee City series.[11] Social scientists labor to define the thing they call "ethnicity." Even the most sophisticated and experienced of them stumble in the effort[12] while those less astute produce little that is useful.[13] I prefer to follow the lead of one authority who reminds the reader that ethnicity is no more than a social construct— a shifting set of definitions of a group by itself or by others. Nagel goes on to confess: "I also use the terms 'race' and 'ethnicity' somewhat interchangeably."[14] She is not alone. Alba and Nee, in their review article on the idea of assimilation, do the same thing.[15]

The models of success described here may in fact have become failures by the time this book appears. As I learned while evaluating social programs, "success" is as dynamic and transient a phenomenon as its counterpart, "failure."[16] The fragility of both Swiss and Swedish models will be noted below. This in no way diminishes the value of such models, which can be demonstrated to have succeeded under certain conditions in certain places at certain times. That such successes, like nearly everything else, may not endure forever is irrelevant to their usefulness. I do not pretend to have discovered in these few instances all of the models which may exist and I urge readers to consider alternatives and to propose additions to this initial collection.

In chapter one I reported how I became involved in such an enterprise. My only qualification was that I had an education and experience as a sociologist with whatever understanding of intergroup relations that implies. Furthermore, I had long been convinced that issues of race and ethnic relations have little to do with science—social or biological—and are almost exclusively moral and political matters. That conviction remains firm. In chapter 1, I told a story that began in Calcutta in early 1989. Graduate students insisted that I discuss with them "Abraham Lincoln and the American melting pot," and they were incredulous when I informed them that the melting pot was not fashionable at this time.

My interest crystallized in Ottawa later that same year. There at the very moment when the Iron Curtain was crumbling everywhere in Eastern Europe, I found myself in the company of a pair of Hungarian sociologists who were less than elated. They explained over coffee that they were Jewish and they feared a resurgent Christian anti-Semitism which lurked barely under the surface in Hungary. Between the students in Calcutta and the Hungarians in Ottawa, I resolved to become engaged in the issue of minority treatment by dominant groups. In chapter 12, I will return to the question raised by the Indian students: Whatever happened to assimilation and where does a policy which encourages ethnic diversity lead?

Let us turn now to a consideration of five possibilities. These suggest that a degree of cautious optimism is justified when policymakers are confronted with intergroup enmities under these specific types of conditions: (1) Ethnic Enclaves; (2) Settler Immigrants; (3) Settler Sojourners; (4) Partition; and (5) the Collapse of Oppressor Power. The national cases which provide the principal bases for this analysis include, among others, Ghana, Switzerland, the Czech and Slovak Republics, Slovenia, South Africa, Sweden, the United States, and Albania.

Notes

1. Harold Orlans, "Edward Shils' Beliefs about Society and Sociology," *Minerva* 34 (1996): 29. The reference is to Edward Shils, *Tradition* (Chicago: University of Chicago Press, 1981), 323.

2. Ronald Cohen, "The State and Multiethnicity," *Cross-Cultural Research* 28, no. 4 (November 1994): 328.

3. Reece McGee in a personal communication, 7 March 2001

4. I am grateful to S. M. Miller not only for his encouragement but for this particular observation that with the vast amount of negative literature on ethnic relations, it would be refreshing to suggest some positive policies.

5. Ashley Montagu, *Man's Most Dangerous Myth: The Fallacy of Race*, 6th ed. (Walnut Creek, Calif.: Altamira Press, 1967), 190, n34. Montagu uses this literature to make his point that race and ethnic prejudice is simply a special case of class prejudice. This is an important observation, which has been neglected in the analysis of contemporary ethnic clashes.

6. Robert Redfield, "Culture Contact without Conflict," *American Anthropologist* 41(1939): 514-17.

7. Redfield cites Ethel John Lindgren, *Anthropologist* (October-December 1938). No

title is provided.

8. John Gillin, "'Race' Relations without Conflict: A Guatemalan Town," *American Journal of Sociology* 53 (1948): 337-43.

9. What I know of the field of conflict resolution is gleaned for the most part from the publications of Louis Kriesberg as well as from his patient instruction in a series of conversations. For a current, informed, and comprehensive analysis of this field see Kriesberg, *Constructive Conflicts: From Escalation to Resolution* (Lanham, Md.: Rowman & Littlefield Publishers, 1998). He is particularly determined to broaden the notion of conflict resolution to include the way conflicts are waged in addition to the way they are settled.

10. Louis Kriesberg, "Preventing and Resolving Destructive Communal Conflicts." in *Wars in the Midst of Peace: The International Politics of Ethnic Conflict*, eds., David Carment and Patrick James (Pittsburgh: University of Pittsburgh Press,1997), 232-51.

11. Arthur M. Schlesinger, Jr., *The Disuniting of America: Reflections on a Multicultural Society* (New York: W. W. Norton, 1992), 42.

12. In the sixth edition (1997) of Ashley Montagu's enduring and definitive work, a variety of definitions appear including, among others, (1) the equation of race and caste, (2) the equation of race and class, (3) the equation of race and ethnicity, and (4) the definition of race as a social construct. There is no inherent inconsistency in these definitions and they may well represent the evolution of Montagu's thinking over the half-century of publication of his volume.

13. Fred W. Riggs, "Ethnicity, Nationalism, Race, Minority: A Semantic/Onomantic Exercise," *(International Sociology* 6, no. 2 (September 1991): 281-305. Part 2 appears in *International Sociology* 6, no. 3 (December 1991): 443-63.

14. Joane Nagel, "American Indian Ethnic Renewal: Politics and the Resurgence of Identity," *American Sociological Review* 60 (December 1995): 947-65.

15. Richard Alba and Victor Nee, "Rethinking Assimilation Theory for a New Era of Immigration," in *Immigration Adaptation and Native-Born Responses in the Making of Americans.* Special Issue of *International Migration Review,* 31(winter 1997): 854, n2.

16. Irwin Deutscher, *Making a Difference: The Practice of Sociology* (New Brunswick, N.J.: Transaction Publishers, 1999), chap. 10.

Chapter 8

The Enclave Solution in Switzerland and Ghana

During a literature search on minority cultures conducted prior to [1985], re-searchers have come up with few references that specifically address policy issues. This in spite of numerous articles and books in the area of "ethnicity," "ethnic relations," and "minority studies." While scholars in these fields . . . often have overlooked direct actions taken by governments regarding the indigenous peoples or immigrant populations.

— David Y H. Wu, 1988: "Introduction: The Issue of National Policies and Minority Cultures in Southeast Asia," *Southeast Asian Journal of Social Science* 16, no. 2 (1988): 2

The Swiss have survived a territorial- and linguistic-based pluralism for centuries without internal violence. They have not necessary liked one another, but as long as the linguistic cantons could remain isolated in their mountain valleys, from one another and from the rest of the world, they found it expedient to tolerate one another. The romantic image of a peaceful Switzerland is widespread. It is seen as a model of reasonable accommodation in a nation composed of people who speak different languages and differ in other cultural characteristics. The policy works among these people who are located in homogeneous communities and are physically removed from one another. The German, French, Italian, and Ro-mansch valleys of mountainous Switzerland provide an ideal setting for such a federation. Outside of Switzerland the myth persists that this is a nation of tolerant multilingual peoples. Nothing could be further from the truth.

Many, if not most Swiss, are not multilingual, nor are they very tolerant. Contemporary Swiss xenophobia is evidenced both in the scientific literature[1] and in recent political shifts to the right, which are strongly flavored with anti-foreigner sentiments and policies. For example, Michael Dreher's Auto Party quadrupled its strength in the Swiss lower house in the October 1991 elections. Mr. Dreher advocates placing immigrants and refugees in well-guarded military camps "until they can be sent back to . . . where they came from." His legislative plans consist of demanding of the government every week, "How many did you expel this week?"[2] In the 1995 elections, 15 percent of the popular vote went to the far right party and, by 1999, 28 percent voted for a far right party. The Swiss far right is isolationist—opposed to immigration and opposed to joining the European Union.[3] I mention this decay of a centuries-old Swiss tradition as a reminder that even successful policies may not endure forever. In fact, Patrick Ireland's study of two Swiss (and two French) cities presents a picture of the Swiss as tending to view immigrants as exploitable commodities to be disposed of when they are no longer needed.[4]

Regardless of its downside, it has also been argued that the Swiss model is unique. Kauffman insists that "Swiss federal democracy is no product for exportation. It is a skilled form of government that has grown up through seven centuries, a flower that may flourish only on the ground of its birth."[5] It is true that during the last decade of the recent millennium there have been peoples who could have benefited from the Swiss model but did not. For example, conditions similar to those in Switzerland were found in multiethnic Bosnia, in Croatia with its Serbian enclaves, and in Azerbaijan with its Armenian enclaves. Yugoslavia chose to purge the province of Kosovar of its majority Albanian-speaking Muslim peoples rather than granting them the degree of autonomy they wanted within the Yugoslav federation.

In truth, there is no reason to believe that any of these peoples have learned anything from the others or see themselves as being in any way similar to the others. There are important differences but there are also important similarities, not the least of which is that the volatile border enclaves are linguistically and religiously related to nations lying directly across the border. This is true of Switzerland as well as Bosnia, Croatia, Azerbaijan, and Kosovo. Unlike the others, the Swiss have been successful in instituting policies that provide local autonomy on local matters. Neighboring peoples do not particularly like each other but under their national policies they do each other no great harm. Is this happy circumstance a peculiar one-time event?

Fortunately, cantonization is not a peculiarly Swiss adaptation, nor is it unique, nor does it require seven centuries to perfect. A more modern version of that solution has emerged successfully in Ghana. In an interview with sociologist J. Max Assimeng, Neil Henry reports that the Chieftaincy Act of 1971 has enabled "Ghana's more than 75 distinct languages and major ethnic groups to be bound peacefully together with the help of some imaginative government policy."[6] The legislation recognizes, on the one hand, the powers of village chiefs in local matters, including the authority to enforce customary tribal law related to such concerns as divorce, land disputes, child custody, and the like. On the other hand, the act retains for the central state responsibility for the military, the judiciary, the economy and other national matters. But there is a third hand which may be crucial. According to Henry the act establishes regional and national assemblies where local chiefs "could discuss and govern their affairs." It is claimed that this system maintains the cultural heritage and identity of the local peoples in the face of a changing society.

There may well be unintended consequences of this third hand. Who is to say that local chiefs, when they meet, must limit their discussion to local issues? Is it not likely that over the years these assemblies may evolve into an independent branch of the government with the authority of the local chieftains acting in concert behind it? In fact there has been at least one effort on the part of a military government to eliminate these assemblies and it was unable to do so. This is one sign of the emerging if unintended power of these groups. I have been told that the act has unified Ghana's once war-prone ethnic groups in an officially recognized national forum.

Ghanaian students I have spoken with in the United States and Ghanaian exiles in Britain confirm this impression. An interview with Kwame Gyeke of the University of Ghana offered further confirmation.[7] An American scholar reassured me that "The Chieftaincy Act seems to be working. I saw it in action in 1995."[8] In 2001 a recently arrived Ghanaian taxi driver in Washington, D.C., offered further confirmation of the effectiveness of the Chieftaincy Act. But it does seem to require constant surveillance. Kramer reported in March 1994 that competition for land in northern Ghana erupted into ethnic fighting that left over 1,000 people dead. Troops from the central government stopped the killing and mobilized food and housing for thousands of displaced people.[9]

Unlike Swiss elections of late and in spite of aberrations such as the one mentioned above, Ghana suggest an enduring quality to the policy. Ghana has a history of military coups, through all of which the 1971 Chieftaincy Act has survived. Also surviving is chapter 22 of the Ghanaian constitution which predates the Chieftaincy Act. It is devoted to spelling out the rights and responsibilities involved in "The Institution of Chieftaincy." Reporting on the December, 1996 reelection of President Jerry Rawlings, James Rupert suggests that "the election appears in many ways to advance Ghana's efforts to build a stable democracy," and "many voters ignored narrow tribal considerations, contrary to voting patterns in many African elections."[10] In the 2000 elections, Rawlings refused to run and his chosen successor did not win. The fact that these results were graciously accepted by the long-time president bodes well for Ghanaian democracy.

More careful analysis of this apparently successful effort to unify a multicultural society may provide useful clues for policy in other societies. This is a model designed to reduce interethnic conflict in nations which have enclaves of groups which are homogeneous and which are somewhat isolated from and hostile toward other enclaves of different homogeneous peoples. It may be that such enclaves will not tolerate a multiethnic urban center in their midst. Croats and Serbs were unwilling to permit Sarajevo to survive, while Swiss urban centers retain their linguistic identities. It might be appropriate for Afghanistan where at this writing (2002) there is still no peace in spite of (or possibly because of) the lack of interest by either Russia or the United States following the end of the cold war and, later, the brief U.S.-led insurrection intended to eliminate terrorists. All of the conditions present in Ghana seem to be present in Afghanistan. Nigeria, a large and populous nation, contains three major ethnic groups which are concentrated in different parts of the country. After years of military autocracies, Nigerians found themselves in the spring of 1999 struggling to reestablish a democratic government. According to Vick,[11] Nigerians refer warily to what has happened to Yugoslavia, Rwanda, and Czechoslovakia, but are they aware of the Ghanaian solution?

Violent and widely publicized negative models are more easily recognized than the less dramatic effective policies quietly practiced by nations such as Ghana. The president of Ethiopia, a nation emerging from years of ethnic and regional violence under a repressive regime, denies that "there will be a repetition of Yugoslavia in this country."[12] Employing similar rhetoric, the K.G.B. warned that ethnic clashes could result in the former Soviet Union "going down the same path as Yugoslavia."[13] Such determination to avoid the negative example is laudable but a positive comparison with Ghana might be more useful. Ethiopia's new national charter could have benefited from a study of the Chieftaincy Act. So too could some of the newly independent republics of the former Soviet Union.

Very different kinds of solutions are required when the minority groups do not reside in homogeneous communities in relative isolation from one another. In the following chapter we will examine a successful solution to another kind of minority situation, the immigrant minority.

Notes

1. Uli Windisch, *Xenophobie? Logique de la Pensee Populair* (Lausanne: Edition L'Age d'Homme S.A.,1978).

2. Stephen Kinzer, "Swiss Voting Results Reflect Anti-Immigrant Mood," *New York Times International,* 27 October 1991, 11.

3. Anne Swardson, "Swiss Vote Reflects Burgeoning Anxieties," *Washington Post,* 27 October 1999, 24(A). Patrick Ireland, *The Policy Challenge of Ethnic Diversity: Immigrant*

Politics in France and Switzerland (Cambridge, Mass.: Harvard University Press, 1994.

4. Ireland, *The Policy Challenge of Ethnic Diversity.*

5. Otto K. Kaufmann, "Swiss Federation," in *Forging Unity Out of Diversity: The Approaches of Eight Nations,* eds. Robert A. Goldwin et.al (Washington, D.C.: American Enterprise Institute, 1989), 206-59.

6. Neil Henry, *Washington Post,* 27 July 1990.

7. Kwame Gyeke, Telephone interview, 4 April 1994.

8. Frank A. Salamone, Personal communication, 2 February 1998.

9. Reed Kramer, "Peace Force in Liberia Threatened," *Washington Post,* 6 March 1994, 29 (A).

10. James Rupert, "Ghana's Voters Give President Another Term," *Washington Post,* 12 December 1996, 43-44 (A).

11. Carl Vick, "Three-Way Ethnic Split Keeps Nigeria Divided," *Washington Post,* 15 July 1998), 1(A) and 20(A).

12. Jennifer Parmelee, "Ethiopia Plies Democracy, Contentiously," *Washington Post,* 22 October 1991, 18(A).

13. Michael Dobbs, "Profits and Loss," a review of *Cafe Europa: Life After Communism* by Slavenka Drakulic in *Washington Post,* 23 March 1997, 8.

Chapter 9

The Immigrant Solution in Sweden, Canada, and Australia

I dream of the day when nobody will hate me because of the food I prefer, my memory, or the language I speak.

—Slavenka Drakulic,, *Café Europa:*
Life After Communism (New York:
W. W. Norton, 1997), 169

Very different kinds of solutions are required when minority groups do not reside in homogeneous communities in relative isolation from one another. Permanent cantonization is certainly less than appropriate in the case of foreign immigrant minorities. Immigration is a complex phenomenon which encompasses a number of different types, but it is so widespread and so troublesome in the contemporary world that it cannot be ignored. I will bypass such disturbing inconsistencies as a U. S. immigration policy which welcomes Cubans but not Haitians—an archaic remnant of both the cold war and racial prejudice.

In contemporary Germany we find that a generous open border policy leads ultimately to resentment and conflict. There are, for example, third generation people of Turkish descent who remain ineligible for citizenship.[1] The Germans might have taken a lesson from the equally homogeneous and nationally older Swedes. They were far more successful than the Germans with an immigrant policy which not only did not deny citizenship to immigrants but encouraged maintenance of their ethnic identity and cultural heritage. Swedish policy appears to be the exact opposite of Swiss, French, and German policy until mid-1999. Let us consider this second successful policy and its consequences.[2] Paulston sets the scene as follows:

At a world standard, Sweden is a very old nation marked until recently by convergent homogeneity of culture and language [with the exception of the Finns and Lapps in the north]. Ask any Swede what the traditional Thursday supperdish is, and he will tell you peasoup and pancakes, and indeed it is a rare cafeteria which won't serve it on Thursday. Into this kind of homogeneity of seven million inhabitants came one million immigrants (it much improved the quality of Swedish cuisine) following World War II, primarily during the sixties and seventies; some were political refugees [from political upheavals in Hungary, Czechoslovakia, and Poland and, later from Chile, Turkey, Vietnam, Uganda, Iran, Poland, and Lebanon] but the majority represented labor market immigration of which the largest groups came from Yugoslavia, Greece, and Turkey.

This is the background out of which Swedish minority policy evolved. I quote at this length because it is necessary to understand the conditions which were dealt with to such a high degree of well-documented success. In 1975 the Swedish parliament established three objectives for immigrant and ethnic minorities: (1) equality between immigrants and Swedes; (2) cultural freedom of choice for immigrants; and (3) cooperation and solidarity between Swedes and ethnic minorities. These sound like little more than benign platitudes, but two years later, the Home Language Reform Act made it the responsibility of municipalities "to provide home language instruction for all students who desire it and for whom the home language represents a living element in the child's home environment."[3] According to Paulston this policy was rigorously adhered to. It would be difficult to imagine any policy better designed and implemented for the purpose of preserving the integrity of immigrant and ethnic cultures. "In fact, it is not happening."[4]

Liljegren has published extensive data on the children who elect to study in their mother tongue. One-third of these children whose parents were both born abroad (second generation) always speak Swedish at home while an additional 20 percent often do in spite of their education in their mother tongue. Furthermore, when we look at those among the home study children whose parents were both born in Sweden (third generation), we find that nearly all of them (94%) always speak Swedish at home.[5] So much for cultural pluralism. I have inserted generational reminders because this third generation phenomenon will reappear in this chapter as well as in chapter 13. If there is any relationship between language and culture, this evidence suggests (as the Chicago sociologists early in the last century predicted) that a pluralist policy benignly administered leads ultimately to assimilation. The Swedish data provide clear confirmation of what Gans calls straight line assimilation—moving through three generations to full assimilation.[6]

Just as there were conditions under which a policy modeled upon Ghana's Chieftaincy Act would be inappropriate, so too certain caveats are required when considering Sweden's pluralist policy. Paulston notes that there are two important exceptions to this trend toward assimilation. Neither the Swedish Gypsies (Roma) nor the Swedish Finns follow this pattern. Since Gypsies are found nearly every-where in the world, and they are likely to be despised by dominant groups wherever they are found, it is important to understand why these people remain apart. Paulston confesses that "I believe the Gypsies will remain Gypsies, just as I believe the great-grandchildren of the Estonians and the Hungarians will become Swedes."[7]

Paulston attributes the failure of rapport between Swedes and Gypsies to the limits of Swedish tolerance. Gypsies are free to choose, but only among alterna-tives that are acceptable to Swedes: "To choose not to send children to compul-sory school is simply not an acceptable choice, however appropriate to Gypsy culture."[8] Paulston does not tell us how it is that the Gypsies are so much more different culturally from Swedes than are many of the other immigrant groups who do assimilate. We can speculate, however, that peoples who are not only pushed from their former environment by economic and political pressures but also are pulled to their new one by a degree of respect and even admiration for the host nation and its people will ultimately move toward assimilation if they and their culture are treated with respect.

Is it safe to assume that Gypsies have no more respect or admiration for Swedish culture than they do for any other alien peoples, all of whom are viewed as polluters of their Romani lifestyle? Gypsies have their own concept of "chosenness." Hancock, an authority on Gypsy history and culture, describes the concept of ritual pollution, "of the *gadze*'s (non-Gypsies) being kept at a social distance by Roma because of a fear that they will contaminate," as having "insulated and preserved Romani identity everywhere."[9]

Observing the Swedish scene two decades later, Runblom writes that the Swedes consider themselves a tolerant people who treat their immigrants with respect. But they are not all happy with the consequences of their benign policy.[10] There have been new waves of immigrants who, like the Roma, do not share Swedish values. These include Bosnian refugees, Turkish "guest workers," and others from south Europe and north Africa. There is, he says, among these more recent immigrants, unemployment, growing disparity in income, and segregation in schools and housing. He also mentions "signs of open hostility"[11]—a central theme found in Pred.[12] Is this because the culture gap is too great or because it takes a few generations for the true consequences of Swedish policy to become apparent? It may be that Gypsies, and perhaps some other immigrants, see themselves as sojourners in a foreign world. But, unlike other sojourners, they have no "home" to return to. This brings us to the Swedish Finns.

Almost half of the pupils with a home language other than Swedish are Finns. Paulston compares Swedish Finns to Puerto Ricans in the United States because of the frequent back-and-forth movement between the original commu-nity and the new one. Note that the Finns are not far from home and are free to migrate and to return at will. It is this constant renewal of ties with their home-land that seems to make the Finns different and unlikely to assimilate to Swedish culture. If the Swedish policy fails in all respects for Gypsies who have little use for the concept of formal schooling, it succeeds in its original pluralist intent for Finns who insist on maintaining their Finnishness.

Finns and Swedes appear to harbor no ethnic grudges. One of the two candidates for Finland's presidency early in 1994 is described as being "from Finland's ethnic Swedish minority, about 6 percent of the population, and [she] leads the small Swedish People's Party." Hockstader suggests that "What is important is that both candidates are seen as "Well-spoken, polite to a fault and well-versed on affairs of state [and] they have run a kinder and gentler race."[13] At least some of this peaceful postwar relationship can be attributed to Swedish ethnic policy.

The sojourner concept is treated in chapter 10. What can be said of Swedish pluralist policy is that it is an effective device for ultimately assimilating minority peoples who have no intention of returning "home." For sojourners it appears to provide a temporary pluralist haven. Note that even the Gypsies, of whom the Swedes disapprove, are not persecuted in that country, regardless of signs of increasing hostility toward new "non-European" immigrants. The conclusion of Paulston's research is that, "Voluntary migration results in much faster [assimilation] than does annexation or colonization" and "Voluntary migration, access to public schools and thus to the national language, and economic incentives in the form of available jobs all contribute to assimilation and language shift."[14] If we did not know she was writing of Sweden in the last half of the twentieth century, we might think Paulston was describing the United States in the last half of the nineteenth century. It would serve the voters of Utah and Arizona well to understand these consequences when they flock to the polls to pass "official language" legislation which the courts must later set aside.[15]

It is ironic that the first decade of the new millennium found the Finns for the first time encountering a sizable number of immigrants. According to Harviainen,[16] Finland is a country with a population of five million and is even more homogeneous than Sweden had been. There appeared at the turn of the century about 85,000 immigrants. Most of them had been in Finland for less than five years. It is in my estimate curious that nations of the world seem oblivious to successful policies contrived by other nations. But, as Alice would have it, it gets curiouser and curiouser.

The neighboring Finns ignore Sweden's successful immigration education policies which benefited Finnish immigrants more than any other group. Instead they take a very different, traditionally American, and potentially more dangerous tack. Harvianen writes that an official goal of Finland's immigrant policy is effective and quick integration into Finnish society: "Immigrants are seen officially as responsible for learning the language and rules of their new society."[17] The Finns appear unwilling to reciprocate the accommodating immigrant policy the Swedes had offered Finnish immigrants. The third largest group of immigrants to Finland are Swedes (the two larger groups are from Russia and Estonia). A final judgment of Finnish policy awaits evidence of its success or failure.

The Swedish case is not the only one to suggest that deliberate multicultural policies facilitate assimilation. Morton Weinfeld documents the history of Canadian multicultural policy, which encourages financially and otherwise the preservation of diverse cultural heritages (in contrast to United States melting pot policies). He then reports the existence of bi-national data demonstrating that assimilation occurs at the same rate in both countries.[18] It is ironic that the collection of essays in which Weinfeld's paper appears advertises itself as a book on "American pluralism," yet nearly every chapter deals primarily with American assimilation.

Truehart independently makes this same observation in his analysis of Canadian immigrant policy: "The Canadian and American immigrant experience over the long haul, raise[s] the question: Is the mosaic ultimately a way station to the melting pot?"[19] Truehart also reminds us that there is considerable self-interest involved in Canada's generous and humane immigration policy. Immigrants and refugees, he claims, keep this vast, thinly populated country from losing population. They also contribute to the tax base and the job pool, and they open lucrative commercial lines to their home countries.

Like Canada but without its liberal immigration traditions, Australia discovered that it was in its own interests to abandon its all-white immigration policy in 1972. In its place Australia now boasts a policy it calls "multiculturalism" which is a sort of separate but equal argument that each ethnic group has something special to contribute to the national entity. Yet, much to the surprise of the Labor Government which set it up, the Fitzgerald Commission reported in 1988 that "Far from fighting to preserve their cultural identity, the ethnic rank and file was aggressively Australian and wanted to stay that way."[20] Again, there is evidence that a pluralist policy results in assimilation. However, the Fitzgerald Report cautions that "The potential for bigotry sleeps within most individuals, and racism in many forms pervades our society."

In fairness to the Germans, they have had one of the most open immigration policies in the world and are providing sanctuary for more refugees from the former Yugoslavia than any other nation.[21] Cohen informs us that between 1990 and 2000, Germany took in close to two million asylum seekers, far more than any other European state. The largest single group were Turks.[22] There is in Germany considerable hospitality toward Bosnian refugees who were taken into homes and otherwise cared for. By July 1992 Germany had already accepted over 200,000 Balkan refugees and was still accepting them. This can be explained in part by German remembrance of their own homeless and foodless conditions following World War II. They see the former Yugoslavs as war refugees—as distinct from the economic refugees whom many Germans despise. An elderly German woman puts it this way: "I remember sitting in the bomb shelters. It hurts even to think about it. These people need to come here; they're not like the other foreigners who make fools of us, coming here to take our jobs and those nice

German social benefits. These are real war refugees—can't you see that?"[23]

This is what the Oliners mean by "extensivity"—the concept of humanity embracing those beyond one's own borders.[24] It is a pity that it could not be extended further to include "those other foreigners." By the spring of 1997, authorities in the state of Bavaria and in Berlin were making plans to repatriate the 320,000 Bosnian refugees, mostly Muslims, by force if necessary. They argued that the war was over and people were supposed to return to their former communities and homes. Besides, the expense of housing and supporting so many foreigners was a heavy economic burden.[25]

Even in the United States, where immigrant policy has not always been consistent, the data is remarkably like the Swedish data. According to Rodriguez's analysis of 1990 census data, "almost half of immigrants from non-English speaking countries reported that they did not speak English proficiently within two years of arriving in the United States. Yet among those immigrants from non-English-speaking countries who had been in the country for thirty years or more, 88 percent said they spoke English well."[26] Rodriguez also informs us that both Asian and Latino immigrants become almost fully assimilated by the third generation. The rates of intermarriage between these immigrant people and Americans of other ethnicity is truly amazing: a third of Hispanic women marry non-Hispanics and the rate is 42 percent for Asian- American women. Further confirmation of this general process can be found in Alba and Nee's review of evidence of assimilation by new immigrant groups. Concluding that the assimilation of second generation groups was only partial, they go on to observe that "It was only with the third and, in some cases, the fourth generations that the powerful undercurrent of assimilation came unmistakably to the surface."[27]

Thus there is evidence from Sweden, Canada, Australia, and the United States that a tolerant pluralist policy which respects the culture and language of immigrants appears to lead directly to assimilation of those immigrants into the dominant culture. This proposition requires two qualifiers. The first is that the erosion of time can wreak havoc with any policy. Just as Swiss tolerance can dissolve, so too can Swedish. One authority claims that there are clear signs of the breakdown of a long-standing humanitarian consensus in Swedish politics.[28]

A second qualifier to the assimilation proposition is that there seem always to be isolated minorities who either are rejected as exceptions, e.g., the descendants of slaves in the United States, or who choose to reject the dominant culture (e.g., Swedish Gypsies and Canadian Francophones). There are also those minorities who view themselves as temporary visitors and harbor some intentions of returning "home" eventually. These are the sojourners who we consider next. It should go without saying that there is little possibility for integration when a nation views immigrants as exploitable commodities to be disposed of when they are no longer needed.

Notes

1. By May 1999, Germany was on the verge of abandoning its archaic citizenship requirements and admitting to citizenship anyone who is German born. The political climate for this shift began to accelerate in the spring of 1997. See William Drozdiak, "Germany Begins to Accept Changing Ethnic Makeup," *Washington Post*, 28 April 1997, 1(A) and 16(A). For the resolution of "Germany's German Question," see Peter Finn's article with that title in the *Washington Post*, 25 November 2000, 16(A). Anyone born in Germany is now a German citizen.

2. Unlike Ghana's Chieftaincy Act, I have extensive documentation of Swedish policy provided by Christina Bratt Paulston in a paper (1988) and a report (1982). The paper is "International Perspectives on Multilingualism and Language Policies" (paper read at the Conference on Language and Ethnicity, Baku, Azerbaijan, June 1988. The report is *Swedish Research and Debate about Bilingualism: A Report to the National Swedish Board of Education* 9 (Stockholm: National Swedish Board of Education, 1982). The following observations are derived largely from Paulston's work.

3. K. Hyltenstam and L. Arnberg, "Bilingualism and Education of Immigrant Children and Adults in Sweden," in *International Handbook of Bilingualism and Bilingual Education,* ed. Christine Paulston (New York: Greenwood Press, 1988).

4. Christina Bratt Paulston, "International Perspectives."

5. T. Liljegren, "Compulsory School Leavers in 1979 with Home Languages Other Than Swedish," *Interim Report #3.* (Stockholm: National Swedish Board of Education, 1981).

6. Herbert Gans, "Introduction," in *Ethnic Identity and Assimilation: The Polish Community,* ed. N. Sandberg (New York: Praeger, 1973). Gan's conclusions are based on his study of an Italian ghetto in Boston. The study was originally published in 1962. See Herbert Gans, *The Urban Villagers: Group and Class in the Life of Italian-Americans* (Glencoe, Ill.: The Free Press, 1982).

7. Paulston, "International Perspectives."

8. Paulston, "International Perspectives."

9. Ian F. Hancock, "Review of *'The Gypsies'* by Angus Fraser," *Contemporary Sociology* 23 (1994): 61-62.

10. Runblom provides a more recent and accessible source of Swedish immigration policy, including the constitutional changes of 1974 and the Home Language Act of 1975. See Harald Runblom, "Swedish Multiculturalism in a Comparative European Perspective," *Sociological Forum* 9, no. 4 (1994): 623-40.

11. Runblom, "Swedish Multiculturalism," 625.

12. Allen Pred, *Even in Sweden: Racisms, Racialized Spaces, and the Popular Geographic Imagination* (Berkeley: University of California Press, 2000).

13. Lee Hockstader, "Few Issues Divide Two [Norwegian] Candidates for Presidency," *Washington Post*, 3 February 1994.

14. Paulston, "International Perspectives."

15. According to an Associated Press release, dateline Salt Lake City, 1 December 2000, "Twenty-six other states are promoting this kind of statute."

16. Lotta Harviainen, "The Finnish Perspective on Immigrants' Identity and Adaptation to a New Culture" (paper presented at the Conference on International Perspectives on Race, Ethnicity, and Intercultural Relations, Oxford, Mississippi., April 2001).

17. Harviainen, "The Finnish Perspective."

18. Morton Weinfeld, "Canadian Jews and Canadian Pluralism," in *American Pluralism and the Jewish Community,* ed. Seymour Martin Lipset (New Brunswick, N.J.: Transaction Publishers, 1990), 87-106.

19. Charles Truehart, "O Canada! . . . Whose Canada?" *Washington Post,* 5 May 1996, 1(A) and 27(A).

20. Russell Spurr, "Australia Goes Asian," *New York Times Magazine* (4 December 1988): 46-49, 52 and 56.

21. As of April 1993 (pre-Kosovo) the U.N. High Commission for Refugees reported that Germany was sheltering 300,000 of the then 643,205 refugees from the former Yugoslavia in Europe. Switzerland was second with 80,000. At that time there were another 271,000 Bosnian refugees in Croatia and 302,000 in Serbia and Montenegro (*Washington Post,* 14 July 1993, 15[A]).

22. Roger Cohen, "How Open to Immigrants Should Germany Be?" *New York Times,* 13 May 2001, 9(NE).

23. Mark Fisher,"In Germany, Welcome Mat For Refugees," *Washington Post,* 31 July 1992, 16(A) and 23(A).

24. Samuel Oliner and Pearl M. Oliner, *The Altruistic Personality: Rescuers of Jews in Nazi Europe* (New York: Free Press, 1988).

25. William Drodziak, "Germany Escalates Drive to Repatriate Bosnians," *Washington Post,* 3 April 1997, 28(A).

26. Gregory Rodriguez, "It Only Takes a Generation or Three," *Washington Post,* 4 July 1999 (3B).

.   27. Richard Alba and Victor Nee, "Rethinking Assimilation Theory for a New Era of Immigration," in *Immigrant Adaptation and Native-Born Responses in the Making of Americans,* Special issue of *International Migration Review* 31 (winter 1997): 850.

28. Robert Miles and Dietrich Thranhardt, eds., *Migration and European Integration: The Dynamics of Inclusion and Exclusion* (Cranbury, N.J.: Fairleigh Dickenson University Press, 1995).

Chapter 10

Sojourner Finns, Israelis, and Greeks and Also the Unfashionable Solution of Partition (India, No! Czechoslovakia, Yes!)

> In the nasty game of musical chairs that followed the breakup of the Ottoman Empire, the Kurds have been left standing.
>
> —Carole O'Leary, "A No-Fly, Yes-Democracy Zone,"
> *Washington Post*, 15 July 2001, (B2)

> The efforts of the U.S. government and others to get people to live in multinational and multiethnic communities are more often than not exercises in futility. Instead, it is often wise to accommodate those pushing for ethnic separation, segregation and homogenization—even if that means partitioning entire nations to reduce violence.
>
> —Samuel P. Huntington, "Will You Become Your Own Nation?"
> *Time* 155, no. 21 (22 May 2000): 113

Sojourners

In chapter 9 we discussed the immigrant solution. Unfortunately for the policy maker, not all immigrants are the same. In fact, there are very different *types* of immigrants. The immigrants whom I consider in this section are quite different from the refugees and others who left their homelands behind to seek a better life in a new nation. The concept of the sociological sojourner has been around at least since Siu employed it in his 1952 analysis of Chinese immigrants to the United States.[1] Siu based his concept on the earlier notions of the Marginal Man and the Stranger.[2] The concept makes an important and useful distinction for policymakers, since peoples who define themselves as temporary visitors require policies that differ from other immigrants and from other types of minorities. The most familiar sojourners are visiting students, refugees, migrant workers, and tourists. On the surface it seems simple enough for governments to deal with such transient populations. But the matter is more complex than it appears: there are students, refugees, workers, and tourists who never do return home.

The Swedish educational policy worked in unintended (although not undesirable) ways for most immigrants. For the Finns in Sweden, however, the policy worked precisely as intended. These people from a neighboring country came to Sweden only to find work which was unavailable at home and with every intention of returning home. They segregated themselves from the local population and made frequent visits to their homeland. Not only were they eligible for most of the generous benefits of the then Swedish welfare state, but in addition that state provided their children with education in their home language—an education which incorporated Finnish culture and history. Unfortunately not all sojourners can expect to find themselves in so benign a milieu.

There is in the definition of sojourners a double layering of subjectivity. Not only are ethnic groups social constructs but sojourners add to that self-definition a second one involving intentions. Intentionality is an important legal and social scientific concept. It is also an amorphous one. What people honestly intend and what they actually do may not be the same.[3] Visiting students and migrant workers may come for a semester or a season and stay for a lifetime. Uriely has explored this double layering of subjectivity among Israeli immigrants in Chicago.[4] Karpathakis in her study of Greek sojourners in Astoria, New York, is able to report comparisons between those who stay and those who do not. Her work is rich in descriptions of the contempt in which older Greek immigrants hold the more recent ones. This is due in part to the self-image of recent immigrants as transients. The older generation is more Americanized and, according to Karpathakis, does not have a good sense of recent historical changes in Greece. She distinguishes clearly between sojourners and settlers.[5]

Uriely makes the same distinction between "settlers" and "sojourners." "However," he writes, "I give close attention to Israeli immigrants who compromise on what I label as a 'permanent sojourner' type of orientation. I argue that 'permanent sojourners' express a unique form of ethnicity which I call 'rhetorical ethnicity.'"[6] As much as the term "permanent sojourner" may sound like an oxymoron, it is not. Uriely discovers a type of objectively permanent settler, who persists in speaking as if he or she is a sojourner. Such immigrants may honestly think of themselves as temporary. The fact that they fail to return home has policy consequences. Is there a reasonable and humane way for a nation to deal with sojourners? What would seem to work is again a policy such as that embedded in the Swedish home language legislation which allows for both the assimilation of those who remain and the retention of home culture for those who return.

The laissez-faire or "sink or swim" policy in America at the turn of the twentieth century toward all immigrants may have achieved that same end.[7] Immigrants poured in and for the most part settled in urban ghettos where familiar cultural surroundings were re-created. This was done with very little help either public or private and the process was surely not as painless as the supportive Swedish policy. The generational shift toward the dominant culture was, however, as remarkable in the United States at that time as it was in Sweden nearly a century later. Little is known of the European sojourners of that earlier period—those who did in fact return to their former homelands. But those who remained moved, generation by generation, to the more distant suburbs and were mostly assimilated into the larger society. The residual ethnic populations who were too old or otherwise not sufficiently competent remained in the original ghettos. It was such residual populations that Glazer and Moynihan studied and from which they concluded that the melting pot had never happened.[8] That flawed research continues to reenforce the myth and provides illegitimate support for contemporary multi-culturalist arguments. I will return to the American condition, especially that of the United States and of Canada, in chapter 13, which deals with the policy implications of the assimilation-pluralist dichotomy.

We have seen that the sojourner is different from the immigrant who intends to remain, and thus different policies are required to meet the needs of this type of immigrant. The Swedish educational policy remains a model. In addition to the enclave situation, the immigration one and the sojourner, we turn to a fourth situation which requires yet another kind of solution. Let us consider partition as a way of dealing with ethnic differences within a nation.

Partition

The most extreme pluralist solution occurs when one nation becomes two (or more as in the case of the former Soviet Union) or part of a nation separates into a new nation. As the example of the Czech and Slovak division suggests, it is possible to accomplish this peacefully and to the mutual satisfaction of both parties. Reports from Czechoslovakia were devoid of signs of violence, with words like "feud" being employed to describe the differences between the two major regions that made up that country.

From the American press one got the impression of a younger sibling (Slovaks) attempting to assert its independence from a domineering and protective older brother (Czechs). In fact, much of the competitiveness between the two was described at first as related to changing the name of the country to emphasize their separateness. Protesters in Bratislava complained of the "arrogance" of the Czech majority. When one talked to people in Bratislava about these matters they did not seem trivial. Yet the "velvet revolution" brought with it a sense of warmth and good feeling. At that time I found myself standing beside a reporter watching the inauguration of President Havel in Prague. Referring to the recently deposed Soviet puppet, she said with tears in her eyes, "we used to be so ashamed of our president." The reporter was a Slovak from Bratislava, not a Czech from Prague, but it made no difference. The Soviet oppressors were gone.

The quarrel between Czechs and Slovaks, unlike many others, did not turn on unequal wealth, political power, or cultural repression. Czech policy has traditionally been one of helping raise the living standards of Slovaks who had, like the Romanians, been ruled by oppressive Hungarian landlords. Nevertheless Slovak feelings ran strong. All fifteen of the parties competing for Slovak votes in federal and regional elections early in June 1990 advocated increased autonomy from Prague for the Slovak Republic. At least one political leader saw a potential for more serious difficulties. According to Milan Simecka (in an interview with Michael Z. Wise),

> Subconsciously within this movement all the dark features of European national-ism emerge. These are a rather reserved position towards Czechs, a highly developed hostility against the Hungarian national minority as well as hostility to all so-called foreign or alien elements, blatant antisemitism, blatant fascism and everything else [deplorable] we know from history.[9]

In the spring of 1997 I scoffed at these dire predictions. I argued that they had so far failed to materialize, although I was aware that anti-Hungarian, Jewish, and Gypsy feelings persisted in the Slovak Republic.[10] Two years later a troublesome and possibly infinite regression in intergroup relations appeared: Czechoslovakians were delighted to be liberated from their Soviet oppressors; then Slovaks were delighted to be liberated from what they perceived to be their Czech oppressors. Four years later the infinite regression had proceeded a step further with persecution of Gypsies being officially sanctioned in the Czech Republic, which was encouraging them to flee to the promised land of Canada in order to avoid brutality at home. Simultaneously, in Slovakia, state-sponsored animosity toward the large Hungarian minority is fanned by nationalist leaders under the guise of a "language law."[11] This kind of forced integration is an example of the dark side of assimilationist policy which is elaborated in chapter 13.

Of immediate importance is the fact that *when a border is defined in terms of linguistic and ethnic differences and when it is accepted by both sides; when there is a common tradition of joint action against common enemies; when there is no history of mutual violence; when it is the less economically viable of the two parties which is most adamant in demanding separation; and when there is a history of democratic ideology among the peoples of the more powerful group—when all of these factors are present, a peaceful division into two national entities can result.* Whether all of these factors are necessary is not clear.

One might consider, although most of these criteria are absent, would such a solution be possible in Sudan, which is a very large country with clear ethnic division of peoples between north and south? In fact, nearly all national borders on the African continent are a colonial heritage and an arbitrary one at that. Peter Lyon argues that the map of Africa is indeed a fragile one: "We're at the end of a hundred-year-old cycle that started with the Conference of Berlin in 1884, when the colonial powers drew up the map of Africa."[12] Ironically, independent African states have held the former colonial borders inviolable. This is a guiding principle of the Organization of African Unity (OAU). The only explanation Lyon can come up with is that "the OAU accepted these boundaries not out of any great love for them, but mainly because the alternatives were just too horrendous to bear."

Most of the conditions specified earlier also fail to be met in the Kurdish area of northern Iraq. Yet when one studies the reports of scholars such as O'Leary, the feasibility of partition becomes apparent. O'Leary does not propose partition but she does write of the importance of the no-fly zone and the establishment of a safe haven for the Kurds in this area where "democratic institutions are beginning to flourish." There have been, she writes, free and fair elections in two provinces in which at least fifteen political parties participated with the assistance of and under the watchful eye of international observers. She describes the Kurdish situation as follows:

> The oil-for-food money that has been misused in the rest of Iraq is being put to good use in Iraqi Kurdistan. There are no starving babies there; satellite dishes, banned in Saddam's Iraq, sprout from the roofs of mud brick houses in Kurdish villages; and Internet cafes are proliferating as the populace gamely embraces globalization.[13]

Does it not seem reasonable that such an area, freed of the oppression of Iraqi rulers who have used both germ and chemical weapons against its civilian populace, is a proper candidate for partition? Is it not possible that Iran and Syria and even Turkey might applaud and support such a solution?

In Canada, unlike Africa and Kurdistan, all of the criteria are present. Should differences between francophone Quebec and the rest of Canada become irreconcilable, this might be the most appropriate solution. Within a year after their "divorce" as one analyst calls the Czech and Slovak breakup, it was described as "a study in civility." Maas observes that differences were settled at a bargaining table rather than on a battlefield and that the Czechs continue to view it in their own self-interest to support the Slovak Republic as a buffer against the volatility of the Balkans to the south.[14] For their part, the Slovaks have enough problems to deal with without causing trouble with their Czech neighbors. At this writing, the peaceful division has survived for over a decade and there is no sign that it will not remain a permanently peaceful one.

Slovenia managed to achieve its independence from Yugoslavia with little more than a symbolic protest from the dominant Serbian government. In contrast with Croatia, Bosnia, and Kosovo, nationalistic Serbian communities did not exist in Slovenia. Furthermore, there could be no border dispute between the two since Croatia lay between them. It may be these factors which account for the relative ease of division in spite of considerable enmity between the two parties. This case does suggest the possibility that even when the more powerful of the two is hostile to the separation, it can occur peacefully.

The conditions enumerated above are many and complex and it is unclear how many of them in what combinations are necessary to achieve a peaceful separation. In fact, the fate of minorities remains ambiguous in Slovakia as does its relationship with Hungary, which is concerned about the large Hungarian minority in that new country. Should Quebec ultimately become a new nation, it would be in a position similar to Slovakia. The concerned minorities in Quebec include all Anglophones but especially Jews who have been rapidly abandoning that province in the face of increasingly open anti-Semitism.[15]

Dividing nations can be a devastating experience with long-range and dangerous consequences. The example of the partition of India and Pakistan provides a horror story of massive population displacements and massacres along with the long-term enmities and dangers to world peace which followed. In India, both Hindu and Muslim intellectuals tell me that partition was a terrible mistake resulting from the insistence of the British overlords who were influenced by a small militant Muslim elite. The Indian writer Salman Rushdie views the violence of March 2002 when a train carrying Hindus was torched by a Muslim mob as a direct continuation of the Hindu-Muslim violence which followed partition over fifty years earlier. Rushdie writes that "Hindu fanatics have been looking for this fight. The pity of it is that some Muslims were ready to give it to them." Rushdie angrily strikes out at religion as the motivating force:

> in India, as elsewhere in our darkening world, religion is the poison in the blood. Where religion intervenes, mere innocence is no excuse. Yet we go on skating around this issue, speaking of religion in the fashionable language of "respect." What is there to respect in any of this, or in any of the crimes now being committed almost daily around the world in religions dreaded name.[16]

A final warning lies in the enduring examples of failure provided by Ireland with borders drawn by treaty in 1921 as well as Cyprus (1974) and Kashmir (1949) whose borders are the result of wars.[17] These cases remind us that without the necessary conditions, the division of one nation into two can result in anything but peaceful consequences and can have long term-repercussions.[18] The major objections to partition lie in the diplomat's distaste for creating more and smaller nations and in the truth that, in Rosenfeld's words, "there is no efficient and painless transfer of populations."[19] Restatements of the traditional arguments against partition appear in Spencer and in Schaeffer.[20] The partition of India clearly supports their position. But the partition of Czechoslovakia just as clearly demonstrates that when the conditions I have delineated are met, the process can indeed be efficient and painless. And most important, *nobody gets hurt.*

It is curious that the term "Balkanization" should carry such negative connotations among scholars, policy makers, and politicians. In a review of Mackey's book on Iraq,[21] Roberts muses over why Mackey avoids this solution. He reminds us that the establishment of a Kurdish state in the north (and possibly a Shi'ite Mulim state in the south) is a logical solution to the situation described by Mackey. "Like various secretaries of state forced to answer for America's brutal treatment of Iraq," Roberts writes, "she can never really say what there is to fear in a balkanization."[22]

In this chapter I have considered two kinds of national policies which appear to work under specified conditions in preventing ethnic groups from doing harm to one another. We saw in chapter 8 that Enclaves can work. Chapter 9 illustrates how respect for the culture of settler immigrants by their host country also works. In this chapter that same policy appears to work when dealing with sojourner immigrants. Finally, we have seen that partition, unpopular as it may be in diplomatic circles, is an effective solution under some conditions. There remains one more kind of successful policy to consider. Reconciliation may be the most difficult of all to implement. But it too works under some conditions.

Notes

1. Paul C.P. Siu, "The Sojourner," *American Journal of Sociology*, 58 (1952):34-44.

2. On the marginal man see, Everett V. Stonequist, *The Marginal Man: A Study of Personality and Culture Conflict* (New York: Charles Scribner's Sons, 1937). On the stranger see, Georg Simmel, "The Stranger" in *The Sociology of Georg Simmel*, ed., Kurt H. Wolff, (Glencoe, Ill.: The Free Press, 1950). Uriely makes a crucial distinction between the two. The marginal man is a failed assimilationist rejected by both the original and the new culture. The Stranger on the other hand is a contented outsider who enjoys the detached role permitted by belonging to no local culture. See Natan Uriely, "Rhetorical Ethnicity of Permanent Sojourners: The Case of Israeli Immigrants in the Chicago Area," *International Sociology* 9, no. 4 (December 1994): 431-45.

3. With the help of my colleagues, I have analyzed evidence related to this discrepancy elsewhere. See Irwin Deutscher, Fred P. Pestello, and H. Frances Pestello, *Sentiments and Acts* (New York: Aldine de Gruyter, 1993).

4. Natan Uriely, "Rhetorical Ethnicity." Uriely provides citations to reports on Chinese sojourners in America (J. W. Loewen, *The Mississippi Chinese: Between Black and White* [Cambridge, Mass.: Harvard University Press, 1971]), Yemeni immigrants in Detroit (J. C. Swanson, "Sojourners and Settlers in Yeman and America," in *Sojourners and Settlers: The Yemeni Immigrant Experience*, eds., J. Friedlander, et.al [Salt Lake City, Ut.: University of Utah Press, 1988]), Indians in Malaya and Burma (U. Mahajani, *The Role of Indian Minorities in Burma and Malaya* [Bombay: Vora, 1960]), Indians in

South Africa (G. D. Klein, "Sojourning and Ethnic Solidarity: Indian South Africans," *Ethnic Groups* 8 [1990]: 1-13), and Indians and "coloreds" in southern Africa (F. Doston and L. Doston, "Indians and Coloreds in Rhodesia and Nyasaland," in *Minorities in a Changing World*, ed., M. L. Barnes, [New York: Knopf, 1967]).

5. Anna Karpathakis, "To Return or to Stay? Factors of Sojourning among Greek Immigrants of Astoria, New York" (paper presented at the annual meetings of the American Sociological Association, Cincinnati, Ohio, August 1991).

6. Natan Uriely, "Rhetorical Ethnicity," 431.

7. My remarks on American policy are limited to European immigrants. Immigration of Asians was severely restricted well into the twentieth century. African Americans, most of whose ancestors arrived in this hemisphere prior to those of European Americans, are a major exception to anything one might observe about immigrants to North America. Imported against their will as slaves and then suffering from massive discrimination and prejudice during the Jim Crow years, these Americans did not obtain their full rights under the law until very late in the twentieth century. Racial prejudice remains endemic in the United States although discrimination has been largely contained.

8. Nathan Glazer and Daniel Patrick Moynihan, *Beyond the Melting Pot: The Negroes, Puerto Ricans, Jews, Italians and Irish of New York City* (Cambridge, Mass.: M.I.T. Press, 1963).

9. Michael Z. Wise, *Washington Post,* 8 June 1990.

10. Irwin Deutscher, "From Time to Time and Place to Place: Ethnic Policies That Work" (paper presented at an international conference on Global to Local Governance, Chania (Crete) Greece, 28-31 May 1997).

11. Christine Spolar, "Slovak Leader Fans Bias toward Hungarian Minority," *Washington Post,* 30 November 1997), 23(A).

12. Peter Lyon, Institute of Commonwealth Studies, London. Cited by *Washington Post,* 25 March 1991) 29(A).

13. Carole O'Leary, "A No-Fly, Yes-Democracy Zone," *Washington Post,* 15 July 2001, 2(B).

14. Peter Maas, "After Their Civil Divorce, Czechs and Slovaks Are Still Friends," *Washington Post,* 10 August 1993, 12(A).

15. Howard Schneider, "Montreal Jews' Anxious Future," *Washington Post,* 29 October 1996.

16. Salman Rushdie, "Slaughter in the Name of God," *Washington Post,* 8 March 2002, 33(A).

17. Karl E. Meyer, "Let's Have Early Imaginative Peace-Work," *International Herald Tribune,* 31 March 1993).

18. For a set of essays describing various cases of national divisions and proposing solutions for easing and preventing this process see Spencer. Some of these essays express concern for what I have described as an infinite regression in the process. Meta Spencer, ed., *Separatism: Democracy and Disintegration* (Lanham, Md.: Rowman & Littlefield, 1999).

19. Stephen S Rosenfeld, "The Partition Fantasy," *Washington Post,* 23 September 1999, 31A).

20. Meta Spencer, ed., *Separatism* and Robert K. Schaeffer, *Severed States: Dilemmas of Democracy in a Divided World* (Lanham, Md.: Rowman & Littlefield, 1999).

21. Sandra Mackey, *The Reckoning: Iraq and the Legacy of Saddam Hussein,* (New York: Norton, 2002.

22. Paul William Roberts, "His Way," *Washington Post Book World*, 2 June 2002, 3.

Chapter 11

Leave Vengeance to the Lord:
One Tough but Grand Solution

Vengeance is mine, I will repay, says the Lord.

—Romans 12:19

The best that is in us knows that individuals are responsible for this crime— not anonymous masses of people. The best that is in us knows that the guilty deserve to be punished—not those who share their names or their language, their skin color or their religion. It knows that blind hatred corrupts the hater. It knows that the greatest power evil has is to entice the innocent to mimic its practices.

—William Schulz, Amnesty International, September 21, 2001[1]

This book began with some words from Shakespeare's character Shylock who encapsulates the problem with sweet vengeance. Shylock warns, "If you wrong us, shall we not revenge?" and reminds his adversaries, "The villainy you teach me, I will execute." Idealistic revolutionaries from Gandhi to King have understood the destructive power of revenge and its counterpart, the curative power of reconciliation. Yet as Gandhi's bitter lesson in India illustrates, forgiveness does not come easy.

Truth and Reconciliation

The principle of reconciliation may have been established in Argentina in the early 1980s. It may have been first codified into formal policy in Chile in 1990. And it may have gained its greatest worldwide attention in Desmond Tutu's Truth and Reconciliation Commission which began its gruesome hearings in South

Africa in 1997. But it was displayed with quiet courage in 1990 when the last of the former Iron Curtain countries of Eastern Europe ousted its long-entrenched Stalinist regime. It is ironic that Albania, isolated and poverty stricken, should have been able to avoid tribal and political violence by renouncing vengeance—only to fall into anarchy seven years later as a result of misconceptions about the nature of capitalism and democracy. This obscure little Balkan country was once again catapulted into world headlines when thousands of Kosovars fled over the Yugoslavian border in search of refuge from marauding Serbs and NATO bombs. It is probable that having become a NATO base and a center of operation for NGO's seeking to relieve Kosovar suffering, Albania will never again be the country it was.

But the most important piece of political advice in these matters is, as Shakespeare warned, vengeance is self-defeating and self-perpetuating. President Havel pronounced sadly at the division of Czechoslovakia that "we are all victims." There is no end to vengeance. Witness Yugoslavia, Ireland, Rwanda, or the Arab-Israeli conflict. In 1990, Albania had an opposition which recognized this. They understood the potential for ethnic and religious conflict after the tyranny was gone and they knew of the dangers of vengeance and retaliation. Albanian Catholics, Muslims, and Orthodox worked together. The opposition announced that:

> Albanians still have vestiges of a clan mentality. Hoxha united Albanians and stopped the custom of blood feuds, which obligated a family to exact vengeance for any bloodshed. To avert a resurgence of these feuds and to prevent a chain of retaliation in this small country . . . the Democrats have called for cooperation with the Communists. Our party is the first to appeal for national forgiveness, for guarantees that no one will seek revenge.[2]

It is on a basis such as this that national and international policies leading to democracy and intergroup justice can be built. The Albanian opposition remained true to its word. On July 3, 1994 a Reuters release from Tirana announced that Ramiz Alia, Albania's last communist leader, along with nine other former Communists was convicted of abuse of power and other charges. Jail terms ranged from three to nine years. Hoxa's widow, arrested in 1991, was also convicted on corruption charges and sentenced to a prison term. If a small, economically deprived, agricultural country with a multiethnic population can dispose of its past peacefully and legally, it may be possible for other nations to do so.

On the other hand, although Albania managed its political transitions without ethnic violence, Battiata observes that, by March 1992, the word "anarchy" was already being used to describe the increase in violent crime and looting which culminated in the utter chaos of 1997 when widespread pyramid schemes collapsed along with the life savings of many Albanians. Nevertheless, the opposition Democrats toppled the former Communist Party government in a free election. The Socialists accepted their defeat and Sali Berisha, the leader of the victorious opposition announced that his country would not seek revenge for communist crimes, including the torture of tens of thousands of political prisoners. "The truth is," Berisha said in an interview with Battiata "that there were many terrible crimes committed during the long dark night but," he continued, "it is also true that so many people were involved in them that to search them out would leave no one left to do the searching."[3]

It is ironic that tribal societies sometimes have a better grasp of this principle than their more "developed" counterparts. Blumefeld informs us that,

> The *Sulha* is an Arab recognition ceremony. In its origins, in the desert, the two feuding clans would meet under a white flag. The killer would arrive wearing a red cloth around his neck. After his family acknowledged his act, the clans would reconcile and the killer could remove the red collar.[4]

Nations can, in fact, learn from one another even when the only thing which unites their distinct cultures is a common heritage of human rights abuses. Michael Wise provides a report on a conference of policy makers from Eastern Europe and Latin America in Salzburg in March 1992. Raul Alfonsin, Argentine ex-president, told the conferees: "Our intention was not so much to punish as it was to prevent, to stop what had happened from happening again, to guarantee that never again could an Argentine be taken out of his home at night and be tortured or assassinated by officials of the state apparatus." Wise points out that under these conditions nations face appeals for national reconciliation as well as demands for settling old accounts. He spells out the dilemma caused by prosecuting acts which were not illegal at the time they were committed: "Today's treason is yesterday's patriotism."[5] Maas writes that when the Hungarians attempted to prosecute elderly Communists who had helped crush the uprising of 1956, the court overturned the legislation, ruling that "We cannot judge a previous period of time from the point of view of the present." Maas reports that Arpad Goncz, the opposition leader who defended his former Communist Party tormenters insisted that "there is a difference between penal procedures and exploring the truth. This decision does not mean that we have to give up exploring the truth."[6]

Although a policy of reconciliation cannot claim to solve a nation's problems, it can surely mitigate them. After an extended and bloody civil war ended in Nigeria with the defeat of the separatist Biafrans, Maier reports that, "Nigeria proved that it could set new standards in compassion. The government's policy of 'No victors, no vanquished' was a remarkable achievement and has played a critical role ever since in keeping the country from splitting apart."[7] Nigeria, a nation with rich natural resources and an educated middle class, remains a corrupt, poverty stricken fiefdom of whatever authoritarian leader is placed in power by the most recent military coup. The important thing is that matters might have been much worse and there is hope that they can someday be much better.

South Africa translated these precedents into a formal policy in its controversial Truth and Reconciliation Commission. Under the leadership of Nelson Mandela, South Africa wrestled with what one columnist describes as the issue of our time: "how the newly liberated deal with the crimes of the past." Krauthammer suggests that in establishing a "Truth and Reconciliation Commission," Mandela resolved the dilemma between justice and vengeance faced by war crimes tribunals.[8] The key to this process, as it was established in Chile, is that what is required above all is a full and unimpeachable accounting of the past. It may be that this process, which worked so well in Chile, Argentina, Hungary, Albania and is on its way to success in South Africa, is what President Clinton hoped would occur in Haiti. It did not. Clearly it was NATO's vain hope that something like this could occur in Kosovo. Nevertheless, it provides a model of what is possible. Because it is so clearly articulated, the South African policy is worthy of closer examination. South Africa's Truth and Reconciliation Commission held its first public hearings in April 1996 and concluded its work in May 2001.

The commission had no powers of prosecution, a failing which its critics see as a deletion of justice from the process. But Duke argues that it did offer: (1) Investigations of cases of human rights abuses by both the previous white government and black opposition groups; (2) a protection program for vulnerable witnesses; (3) reparations for survivors; (4) a record of the scope of apartheid-era crimes; and (5) a framework for a national process of forgiveness. Finally, it offered something none of the earlier programs in other countries have: (6) the possibility of amnesty for offenders who come forth and confess.[9]

Amnesty, like the absence of prosecutorial powers, offends many victims and their supporters because it allows self-avowed murderers and torturers to go free. Duke reports that "Once they have received amnesty through the Truth Commission, perpetrators can neither be sued nor criminally charged for abuses. Such amnesties will be granted on condition of a full and truthful confession." There are also white opponents to the commission who fear it will conduct witch-hunts to track down security force members or officials accused of crimes. The life of the commission was clearly spelled out. It would convene for up to two years, investigating abuses that occurred between March 1960 and December 1993. Nearly a year after it was convened, the commission, chaired by Archbishop Desmond Tutu, inspired an American columnist to describe it as,

> extraordinary. The very idea of granting amnesty to agents of what was the world's most universally hated regime—requiring only that they tell the truth about their role in the atrocities—is extraordinary. And only extraordinary human beings like Tutu and the truly astounding President Nelson Mandela, could have any hope of carrying it out in a way that produces a decent amount of both truth and reconciliation.[10]

Note the contrast with the policy pursued by Simon Wiesenthal and other dedicated Nazi hunters who, a half-century after the Holocaust, continue their heroic mission of bringing sick, old, and forgotten villains to trial. Guilt has long since been established. Retribution seems pointless. In contrast, Rasberry believes there are two reasons why the work of the commission was not pointless. "The first is that without [it] most of the murderers would never have been known for sure. The offer . . . for a possible amnesty will at least solve hundreds of unsolved murders." The second is a direct quote from Mandela: "We can now deal with our past, establish the truth . . . Only the truth can put the past to rest." As with other possibly workable policies, this one requires a few caveats. Duke tells us that Chile investigated about 3,000 cases of human rights violations, "and the process resulted in a system of reparations for survivors. Still, political assassinations continued during the work of the commission, proving the fragility of attempts to reconcile with the past."[11] The Argentine Commission documented some 9,000 cases. Duke is of the opinion that its work may have been helped by the simultaneous trials of military officers held accountable for rights abuses.

In chapter 9 our analysis of a well-documented successful policy in Sweden suggests that no solution is permanent and no solution is perfect. In the spring of 2001 I was privileged to participate in a conference in Oxford, Mississippi, which included a full day of presentations by South African scholars and intellectuals. The Truth and Reconciliation Commission was winding down its work and would within a month cease to exist. The most thorough critique among those many disillusioned South Africans came from Clint van der Walt. He reminded us that only human rights violations were considered by the truth and reconciliation commission and only those carried out since 1960. He also pointed out that the commission dealt only with personal narratives and individual acts of physical violence.

But his most telling critique of the Truth and Reconciliation Commission was yet to come: the atrocities exposed by the commission were by and large violations of the apartheid laws which did not sanction murder and torture. As a result, *apartheid as a system remained unchallenged.* The focus was on illegal atrocities.[12] Others of that South African delegation made telling points. For example Heidi Grunebaum is rightly appalled by the claim of the commission to explore the damage done by apartheid on both sides! Somehow in the name of fairness both sides must be treated equally. Perhaps we should, in all fairness, consider the damage done by Jews to the Nazis.[13] It may be that the most prominent perpetrators of the horrors of a previous regime must be brought to justice in order for a nation to proceed with the business of truth and reconciliation. It is also possible that it takes strong moral leadership of substantial integrity as was found in the Albanian opposition and in the new South Africa. These failed to materialize in Haiti or in Kosovo. Integrity and morality such as that of Tutu and Mandela is not easily found in the contemporary world.

Unlike the other solutions reviewed here, this one is widely known. The international publicity attending the South African Truth and Reconciliation Commission is partly responsible. The international conference on this issue also reflects worldwide awareness. In the new millennium, characterized by highly specialized experts, well-informed consultants have appeared. Pricilla Hayner's book, dealing with dozens of examples, describes the different origins and different mandates of such commissions. They do, indeed, appear to vary in many ways, including their relative success and failure in dealing with the issues they address. But Hayner sums it up well in an interview with Boustany: "The act of officially stating the truth, lifts the veil of silence and denial. . . . It changes the nature of what happened."[14]

Summing Up: Policies That Work

The chapters in part 2 reviewed evidence of five national policies which have proven capable of preventing intergroup violence. They are different from one another and they achieve their ends under different conditions. An ever-present danger in an analysis such as this is the conscious or unconscious selection of supporting evidence and the neglect of contrary evidence. I have encountered no evidence suggesting that a deliberate multicultural policy leads to anything other than assimilation. There is also no evidence that a laissez-faire policy, given three generations, leads anywhere but to assimilation. There is evidence that a deliberate assimilation policy can have devastating and enduring consequences.

It is, however, also true that not all assimilation policies are necessarily dark ones. This matter is pursued in part 3. It is also true that not all policies need to be national. That too is pursued in part 3. The policies described in part 2 are my best bets based upon the evidence I have seen. It would be helpful if others sought and found contradictory evidence in order to improve our understanding of the conditions under which certain national policies work in providing all peoples with the protection of and equal access to the privileges and benefits and laws of their own society.

Notes

1. For a full statement of Shulz's position see William F. Schulz, *In Our Own Best Interest: How Defending Human Rights Benefits Us All* (Boston: Beacon Press, 2001).

2. Laura Silber, *Washington Post*, 29 December 1990

3. Laura Blumenfeld, "A Separate Peace," *Washington Post Magazine* (24 March 2002): 16.

4. Mary Battiata, "Albanian Democrats Win in Landslide," *Washington Post*, 23 March 1992, 1(A); and "Albania's Post-Communist Anarchy," *Washington Post*, 21 March, 1992, 1(A) and 18(A).

5. Michael Z. Wise, *Washington Post*, 8 June 1990.

6. Peter Maas, "Hungary Bars Trials for Ex-Leaders," *Washington Post*, 4 March 1992.

7. Karl Maier, *This House Has Fallen: Midnight in Nigeria* (Public Affairs: New York, 2000), xxvi.

8. Charles Krauthammer, "Truth, Not Trials," *Washington Post*, 9 September 1994, 27(A).

9. Lynne Duke, "South Africa Seeks Truth, Not Justice, in Crimes Past," *Washington Post*, 1 April 1996, 1(A); and "Truth Commission Starts Search in South Africa," *Washington Post*, 16 April 1996, 1(A).

10. William Raspberry, "Tears for South Africa," *Washington Post*, 21 February 1997, 21(A).

11. Duke, "South Africa," 17(A).

12. Clint van der Walt, "Race, Historical Compromise and Transitional Democracy in the Truth and Reconciliation Commission" (paper presented at a conference on International Perspectives on Race, Ethnicity, and Intercultural Relations, University of Mississippi, Oxford, Mississippi, 21 April 2001).

13. This is my observation, not Ms. Grunebaum's, although I suspect that, as the daughter of refugees from Nazi oppression, she would agree with my parallel. Heidi Grunebaum, "Where the River Meets the Sea: A Personal Conversation of Memory and Identity in Present-Day South Africa" (a talk presented at a conference on International Perspectives on Race, Ethnicity and Intercultural Relations, University of Mississippi, Oxford, Mississippi, 21 April 2001).

14. Pricilla B Hayner, *Unspeakable Truths: Confronting State Terror and Atrocity* (Boston: Routledge, 2002).

Part 3

Over the Horizon

Chapter 12

Beyond National Policies

We need a global culture of conflict prevention.

—Anna Lindh, Swedish foreign minister

It would be misleading to leave the impression that all policies are national. That is untrue. There is increasing evidence of effective policy on both multinational and local levels. I have not neglected these two dimensions because they are unimportant. There is an apparent trend toward economic and political globalization. Nevertheless, I believe that the nation-state remains at this moment in history the most effective source of policies that can induce the kinds of changes needed. It is my purpose to help create an awareness of what can be done. In this chapter I attempt to recognize the growing importanceof both localand multinational policy efforts to reduce intergroup conflicts.

Greater Than Nations

It was the United Nations which restored enough order in Albania so that another international entity, the Organization for Security and Cooperation in Europe (OSCE), could reorganize the government and establish early elections. It was NATO which put an end to Serbian harassment of ethnic Albanians in Kosovo. In a similar manner, West African nations have made joint efforts to end ethnic violence in Sierra Leone and the Congo. It is becoming increasingly fashionable to argue that the nation-state is obsolete. This may be correct, but it will be a few years before most nation-states are willing to concede their obsolescence.

The new ideology derives in part from movements toward a unified Europe and there is in fact a European Community in existence. The idea of transnational or multinational authority suggests that the thinking in this book may have been too limited in restricting itself to consideration of national policies. The broadest and best known of international organizations, the United Nations, has traditionally held to the position that it must respect the rights of individual nations to deal with their internal affairs as they see fit. It has, until recently, adamantly refused to intervene unless requested to do so by those nations. This stance appears to be eroding. Let us not forget that a goodly portion of what constitutes human rights is ultimately a matter of race or ethnicity. It may be its clear position on human rights that has pushed the UN toward a new view of its role in international affairs.

Cohen argues that national sovereignty is on the decline and that international law and tribunals are emerging to replace it. He is most impressed by the number and variety of covenant agreements about human rights—which I believe consist largely of the rights of ethnic minorities:

> From 1929 to 1980 there were more than thirty international codes of human rights signed by regional and worldwide groups of sovereign state governments. . . . The international community and the United Nations now claim with actual precedence (e.g., the Kurdish case) that the world community has a "right" to override state sovereignty in the cause of universalistic human rights.[1]

This number has surely increased exponentially in the years since 1980. By the early 1990s even so conservative a diplomat as Jean Kirkpatrick questions the traditional UN stance that the treatment of citizens by their government is strictly an "internal matter" in which other nations have no right to interfere. She cites the French secretary of state for human rights "who has spoken insistently of an international 'right to intervene' in cases of massive human rights violations." Kirkpatrick quotes the U.S. assistant secretary of human rights: "human rights problems should no longer be considered as essentially within domestic jurisdiction."[2] Later that same year, citing both the Balkans and Africa, Nye argued that the answer to interethnic violence lies in international protection.[3]

Transnational pressures can be brought to bear effectively without overt interference. Banton insists that the independence of Namibia, Mozambique, and Zimbabwe as well as changes occurring in the Republic of South Africa, "would not have happened so quickly without the creation of an international consensus bitterly critical of racial politics." He sums up the matter this way:

> The era of the nation state has been characterized by appeals to a contentious doctrine of state sovereignty as a way of resisting what governments see as interference from outside. It is noteworthy, therefore, that in such an era international human rights law should have developed so rapidly and jurists can now confidently testify that freedom from slavery, from genocide, from racial discrimination, and from torture, are protected by international law.[4]

More recent events confirm Banton's argument. Positive support by powerful outsiders and their encouragement of human rights can help prevent trouble before it occurs. In December 1993, U.S. vice president Gore praised Kyrgyzstan president Akayev, "for undertaking radical economic reforms, guaranteeing human rights, and moving his country toward multi-party democracy." Smith goes on to tell us that "in pursuing democratization, Akayev has had to keep calm among ethnic groups—including Kirgiz Russians and Uzbeks—fearful of discrimination."[5]

At the very least international organizations have the capacity to influence national policies for the better. The record of Slovakia in its treatment of minorities, especially the Roma Gypsies, is not good. They have tried to export them to Canada by buying them plane tickets and promising that the Canadian streets are lined with gold. But Schneider and Spolar, who have documented this process, note that the intense desire of Slovakia for NATO membership has tempered Slovakian policy. They report that, as that country was positioning itself for NATO membership in 1999, the government announced a new policy to aid its approximately 300,000 Gypsies. The rationale is that this new policy would help integrate Slovakia into the European and world economies.[6]

A few years earlier, a *Washington Post* editorial had praised Slovakia, along with Hungary and Romania. The three countries had peacefully worked out long-standing border problems. According to the editorial it was the lure of membership in the European Union and NATO along with the minority guarantees outlined in the Council of Europe that brought about these remarkable accords.[7]

With the exception of the Asia-Pacific region, the world today is well covered by regional organizations which monitor human rights. At the turn of the century, the Association of Southeast Asian Nations (ASEAN) continued to resist any imposition of sanctions or other restrictions upon the Burmese military junta's continuing rape and murder of ethnic village peoples in that country, or Indonesia's violent repression in East Timor, or even the continuing rampages of the Khmer Rouge against Vietnamese ethnics in Cambodia. Nevertheless, there is evolving both within the UN and outside of it an increasing recognition of international responsibility in matters of human rights violations. In the first year of the new millennium an international court designed to try war criminals began operating in the The Hague. As the year 2001 began President Clinton, in his last days in office, signed on.

Nongovernmental organizations have also been active in seeking peaceful resolutions to interethnic violence. Ottaway writes that in April 1993, the International Research and Exchanges Board succeeded in quietly persuading the Romanian government to accede to many of the demands of its Hungarian, minority including the important ones revolving around language and education.[8] In effect, Romanians of Hungarian descent got their language back. The failure of peaceful international efforts to negotiate a reasonable conclusion to the violence in Bosnia may have provided the world with a lesson on the limits of negotiation—a lesson which it should have learned from Neville Chamberlain in 1939.

As the European Community plan—the Vance-Owen cantonization proposal—evaporated in June1993, French prime minister Eduard Balladur proposed a new forum to ensure respect for minority rights in Eastern Europe. According to Rupert the extensive monitoring and reporting by the Conference on Security and Cooperation in Europe (CSCE) may not have stopped the carnage, but it did document it.[9] That organization continues to work quietly to find a solution to the Armenia-Azerbaijan conflict. And the tardy U.S. intervention (under the guise of NATO) in 1995 brought the violence to a halt for most Bosnians at least for a while.

In June, 1992, Secretary General Boutros Boutros-Ghali proposed a permanent army for the UN empowered to intervene and "hold in check the nationalist and ethnic tensions let loose by the Cold War's end ."[10] By October of that year a more specific proposal had been put forth by the United Nations Association of the United States. By 1994 the UN had begun employing the military power of NATO, first in a successful effort to bring an end to the shooting in Sarajevo, and later to bring relief from bombardment to civilians in Muslim enclaves along the Drina River. In Somalia the UN transcended its peacekeeping and humanitarian aid roles for the first time in an effort to impose democratic order upon that country. It may indeed be that minority policies of the future will be guided by international standards and enforced by international organizations.

As with assimilation (which we shall examine in the next chapter) there is a dark side to globalization. There are of course the facile critiques dramatized by demonstrations against international corporations. But it is also important to take note of what Kaplan and Bjordo see as a trend toward transnational political extremism based on racist ideologies and dominated by young people. They use the term "emulation" to describe the process in which right-wing groups in different countries copy one another. "Penetration" is used to describe direct cross-national communications among such groups. They suggest that penetration is increasing and that the United States is the major source from which right-wing activities and communications flow.[11] Contributing to the dark side is the fact that international efforts sometimes have unintended consequences. They can do harm. For example, as it became apparent in 1997 that Slovakia would likely be denied access to NATO, the Slovaks began looking for someone to blame and they blamed Prague. Spolar reports that "excluding Slovakia [from NATO] could create a very bitter black hole in the middle of Europe." The headline reports "With Prague Favored, Bratislava's Angry Meciar Demands Apology for Havel Remark."[12]

The critique of international intervention may be posed as human rights versus cultural rights. According to Branigin, this is the basis on which ASEAN defended its refusal to confront the atrocities of the Burmese junta, Cambodia's Khmer Rouge, and Indonesia's behavior in East Timor. When the West condemned these events, ASEAN defended its policies of "constructive engagement" and "quiet diplomacy." Branigin writes that over a quarter of a million

Muslims of the Rohinga ethnic minority in Burma have fled to Bangladesh to escape persecution.[13] People must indeed be desperate to flee to one of the poorest nations on earth. Other examples of the issue of human rights vs. cultural rights occur in critiques of the practice of female circumcision in West Africa and women's rights in general in such Muslim nations as Saudi Arabia.

There is another side to international or multinational policies designed to prevent powerful predators from victimizing minority prey. This other side suggests that, in addition to the influence of political units larger than the nation-state, effective action can be taken by political units smaller than the nation-state. Let us explore this option.

Smaller Than Nations

If there is a movement toward globalization in the creation and implementation of policies, so too there is a movement toward local control of policies. This is the other side of the coin. In this volume I have not properly considered the role of communities, cities, and localities in generating their own policies. They are in fact closer to the issues than their distant national capitals. Such local concern and the willingness and ability to mobilize policy around it were clearly evidenced in the gathering of local politicians and ethnic activists from many places in Europe at a conference in Birmingham, England in 1991. In the preliminary announcement for that conference, Sydney Roper wrote that "Local governments throughout Europe are at the very centre of this challenge. It is the local governments who represent the local communities, who provide services peoples need, and who can assist them to overcome disadvantage." On the other hand, this same announcement reminds us that in a recent report on the position of North African immigrants, the Council of Europe says of the host countries in Europe: "Local government, which is closest to the problems, is often unable to cope with them, not only for lack of resources but also because it frequently lacks the courage to work out a local policy for integration of immigrants. . . . it is often the political will which is lacking."[14]

As discouraging as this may sound, it is not universally true. Bill Gray, the Birmingham city councillor who chairs the Community Affairs Committee of that council, was stirred to action by the Birmingham riots. He and other councillors moved to implement equal opportunity in city government employment (quotas are illegal in Britain). Although social scientists are slow to accept the fact that there is a vast gap between attitudes and behaviors[15] politicians sometimes exhibit a native wisdom in such matters. In a hallway chat with Gray, I asked him how they had managed to bring about such quick changes in race relations in Birmingham. He insisted, correctly, that you can't change attitudes and it is a waste of energy to try. Instead, he says, you impose penalties upon people who do not abide by policies: "If they didn't perform in Birmingham—if they didn't hit their targets of minority hiring—then it was good bye! They no longer worked for Birmingham."[16] Birmingham was not the only city to demonstrate that, in spite of fiscal and other limitations, localities can act on their own. Among other cities reporting considerable success were Frankfurt, Graz, and Antwerp.

The brightest examples sometimes appear in the darkest places. In Northern Ireland there is squalor and poverty, seemingly endless death and destruction, and the foot dragging of the Ulster Unionists and Sinn Fein. The Good Friday peace process has been stalemated by those in high places. But, according to Reid, "all over Northern Ireland [from] the Belfast city line to rural valleys, community based movements have sprung up." Many of these local efforts, about 2,000, are organized with the help of a nongovernmental organization (NGO)— the Northern Ireland Voluntary Trust. The trust brought over a million Protestants and Catholics together to form jobs co-ops, Child care centers, and women's centers. And beyond the necessities Reid describes garden societies, hiking clubs, library boards, and music ensembles in which "people are finding that shared interests can overcome long-standing enmities." We are also reminded that the same thing happens in town and village councils where "rank and file members of both parties manage to sit down every day . . . to work on common issues."[17] A local politician and Nobel Peace Prize winner, John Hume, believes that that is where the hope lies in Northern Ireland. Meanwhile Protestant and Catholic leaders won't even shake hands.

Howard Ehrlich proposes an even more complete form of local self-determination—something he calls "social anarchism": "People accept as axiomatic that the interests of the 'state' take precedence over the interests of cultural minorities." In a proposal somewhat resembling the Ghanaian solution, he suggests the reverse of this, namely that any community ought to be able to organize itself and its relationships to other communities, "within specified lawful/contractual relations."[18]

Conclusion

There are, therefore, reasonable arguments for searching for solutions to intergroup violence not only on the national level but also on the multinational and local levels. We have reviewed some evidence which supports this potential. I have proposed five national models for the possible solution of ethnic differences in the contemporary world—five models which sometimes are successful. In retrospect, it becomes apparent that some policies are preventative in that they avoid potential conflicts. Such policies attack the issue before the fact. This is true of the Swedish immigration policy of the 1970s as well as other tolerant policies toward sojourners.

Other policies may be effective either as after-the-fact efforts to correct problems, e.g., South Africa's Truth and Reconciliation Commission, or as anticipatory and preventative, e.g., the Albanian opposition policy of eschewing vengeance. The creation of new borders and the institutionalization of enclaves are both policies which may be either preventative or corrective. There has also been apparent success under at least three other types of conditions which are barely mentioned in this volume. One has to do with policies toward native peoples by settler nations. Increasing information in this area is emerging from Australia, Brazil, Canada, and the United States. I touched upon this in chapter 3 (39-41). The second involves the need to find general conditions under which a successful integration of a large nation consisting of culturally varied peoples can occur as it did in Tanzania and as my Indian students hope for in their homeland.

The third potential for success also appears in Africa where Mozambique is welcoming white refugees from Zimbabwe. With a rationality rarely found among the bitter ex-European colonies, the government of Mozambique sees it in its own economic interest to make large land grants (up to 2,400 acres of fertile farmland) to these experienced farmers who have been ejected from their lands in the neighboring country. Hoagland reports the beginnings of this process which involves less than 100 white farmers in early 2002. He describes this emerging policy as "pragmatic" in a nation where only 5 percent of the arable land is now under cultivation.[19] What form the relationship between whites and blacks will take remains to be seen. If nothing else these small reminders that different peoples can live together in peace should encourage readers to seek additional policies that work. In the final chapter we shall consider some of the values and politics related to the policies we have discussed. But first let us turn to a consideration of the usefulness and timeliness of the concepts of assimilation and pluralism.

Notes

1. Ronald Cohen,, "The State and Multiethnicity," *Cross Cultural Research* 28, no. 4 (November 1994): 333.

2. Jean Kirkpatrick, "It Is Appropriate to Speak of Genocide," *Washington Post*, 2 March 1992.

3. Joseph S. Nye, Jr., "The Self-Determination Trap," *Washington Post*, 15 December 1992, 23(A).

4. Michael Banton, "The Nature and Causes of Racism and Racial Discrimination," *International Sociology* 7, no. 1 (March 1992): 83.

5. Jeffery Smith, *Washington Post*, 13 December 1993.

6. Howard Schneider and Christine Spolar, "Czech Prejudice— and TV—Fuel Gypsy Migration to Canada," *Washington Post*, 1 September 1997, 23(A).

7. Editorial, "Instead of Ethnic War," *Washington Post*, 21 March 1995, 16(A).

8. David B. Ottaway, "Romania Seeks to Ease Ethnic Tensions," *Washington Post*, 3 April 1993, 20(A).

9. James Rupert, "Diplomats on Lonely Mission to Ease Tension in Yugoslav Re-

gions," *Washington Post*, 9 June 1993, 28(A).

10. John M Goshko, and Barton Gellman, "Idea of a Potent U.N. Army Receives a Mixed Response," *Washington Post,* 29 October 1992, 22(A) and 24(A).

11. Jeffrey Kaplan and Tore Bjorgo, eds. *Nation and Race: The Developing Euro-American Racist Subculture* (Boston: Northeastern University Press, 1998).

12. Christine Spolar, 1997. "Bids to Join NATO Put Czech and Slovak at Odds," *Washington Post*, 13 April 1997, 26(A).

13. William Branigin, "Southeast Asians, West at Odds over Rights," *Washington Post*, 26 July 1992, 29(A) and 32(A).

14. Sydney Roper, *Preliminary Announcement of a Conference on Racial Equality in Europe*, Birmingham, England, 3-6 December 1991, 5.

15. For an analysis of the evidence see Irwin Deutscher, Fred P. Pestello, and H. Frances G. Pestello, *Sentiments and Acts* (New York: Aldine de Gruyter, 1993).

16. From notes on a conversation with Gray. See also, William Gray, "The Birmingham Experience" in *Racial Equality in Europe*, Conference Report, ed., Ahmed Khurshid, (Birmingham, England, 1992), 31-32.

17. T. R. Reid, "Northern Ireland's Communities of Hope," *Washington Post*, 23 September 1999, 21(A).

18. Howard Ehrlich, Personal Letter, 22 May 1991.

19. Jim Hoagland, "New Beginnings in Mozambique." *Washington Post*, 10 January 2002, 19(A).

Chapter 13

Assimilation and Pluralism: An Outmoded Distinction?

The brown people inhabiting Smith's England are chiefly involved in assimilating and disappearing into the pink-faced Britannic masses. This is not the African-American slave saga; this is the African as willing migrant to a country of bad weather, bad food and bad, bad white privilege. Assimilation is a goal here, seemingly. Black Brits can and do melt into the pot.

—Esther Iverem in a review of Zadie Smith's *White Teeth*[1]

As ten years of my work drew to a close in the summer of 1999, I presented the paper on which this chapter is based to a gathering of social scientists in Athens, Greece. The occasion was a meeting of a research group of the International Sociological Association. This particular group had been founded by Adam Podgorecki. His central concern was the development of moral means for the use of sociology in the democratic governance of peoples. He created the term "sociotechnics" as a device for distancing his central interests from the negative implications and aura of "social engineering."[2] It was Podgorecki who had invited me to that long ago Ottawa conference mentioned in chapter 1. The Athens occasion was saddened by Podgorecki's recent death. For me it was a particularly mournful occasion for it had been barely ten years since that man had inadvertently set me on the path that led to this volume.

This book reflects Podgorecki's central interests in its effort to rally social science knowledge into policy recommendations designed to bring about moral ends. What he intends by "dark social engineering" is social engineering or "sociotechnics proper which is consciously used to produce harm. It is not technique but rather goals which constitute the difference." I would add that it is not only intentions but also consequences which constitute the difference. His clear identification of the possibility of a dark side is a useful cautionary for social scientists who dabble in politics and policy. Podgorecki uses Nazi Germany and Communist Poland as examples of the dark side of social scientific applications. More recently the concept of "ethnic cleansing" appeared as a Serbian application of social science in Bosnia and Kosovo. The concept was readily borrowed by Bosnian Croatians and by Kosovars who turned it back on its originators. Need I again remind the reader of Shylock's warning?

In the United States today there are so called "think tanks" funded by conservative sources and supporting social scientists who sometimes produce work on the dark side. Herrenstein and Murray's *The Bell Curve*[3] comes to mind. It deals with race or ethnicity which is what this book is about. For a complete analysis of that work within the historical context of its predecessors, I refer you to Ashley Montagu's 1997edition of *Man's Most Dangerous Myth: The Fallacy of Race.*[4]

In chapter 3 I identified the range of historic national policies toward minorities. Some of these, as politically and economically expedient as they might be, are indeed very dark. They are so on purely moral grounds. I have excluded from my discussion slavery or any form of forced labor, expulsion, annihilation, or physically removing and caging minorities on reservations. Although I do not know of anyone who argues that it benefits minorities to be killed, enslaved, or exported, there are those who argue that it is beneficial for indigenous minorities for the dominant group to isolate them in zoos. I will touch on this matter again at the close of this chapter.

Having ruled out certain dark solutions to intergroup relations, I set out to seek national policies which appeared successful in their efforts to keep groups from doing harm to one another on the basis of their ethnicity. In part 2 I described five such national policies and the conditions under which they appeared likely to be effective elsewhere. All of these lie somewhere on the continuum between extreme assimilation (referred to as "absorption" by Californians and Israelis) and extreme pluralism (the Canadians call it their "mosaic" while elsewhere the terms "diversity" and "multicultural" are employed). This chapter constitutes an essay on the unexpected conclusions to which my earlier work has led. We are not yet finished with the dark side. Those conclusions will demand that we beware of it!

In the rhetoric of postmodern sociology, the distinction between assimilation and pluralism is an anachronism which needs to be discarded. It is an antique discourse. Nathan Glazer asks, "Is assimilation then dead?" He answers: "The word may be dead, the concept may be disreputable, but the reality continues to flourish."[5] The evidence presented in this chapter from various places and various times suggests that he is correct, although I believe that the word remains alive and the concept is useful regardless of its repute. Although lonesome in my view, I am not alone. Richard Alba and Victor Nee, for example, insist that although the term "assimilation" is in bad repute, "assimilation theory has not lost its utility [for research purposes]."[6] It is true that one of the five successful policies, the Ghanaian Chieftaincy Act, is clearly multicultural. But another of the five successful national policies I discovered raises interesting questions about that antique discourse. Let us reconsider the Swedish Home Language Reform Act of 1977.

A quick review of some of the data In chapter 9 is necessary for the present consideration of the notions of assimilation and pluralism. We saw there that the act made it the responsibility of municipalities "to provide home language instruction for all students who desire it and for whom the home language represents a living element in the child's home environment."[7] If one intended to devise a policy designed to preserve the integrity of immigrant and ethnic cultures, the Swedish Home Language Reform Act would provide a prototype. But the data reviewed in chapter 9 document the exact opposite result. As we move from a generation of children whose parents were both born abroad to those whose parents were both born in Sweden, we find that nearly all of the children end up speaking nothing but Swedish at home. So much for cultural pluralism.

If there is any relationship between language and culture, the evidence from this one case suggests that a pluralist policy benignly administered leads ultimately to assimilation. There is other evidence suggesting the same conclusion. We saw in chapter 9 that data from the 1990 U.S. Census show Asian and Latino immigrants to the United States, assimilating at the same three generation rate as did the Swedish immigrants. Independant confirmation of the Census data is found in a nationwide survey of 2,800 Hispanics reported in 1992. Most of these respondents prefer to think of themselves as Americans. Reflecting the larger society, nearly all of them said that Hispanics should speak English and over half grumbled that there were too many immigrants in the United States.[8]

There is further evidence, this time from Canada, that deliberate multicultural policies facilitate assimilation. Canadian policy is a glorification of diversity. Schnieder uses a public school in Toronto's working class west end as an example. Here he reports that students are immersed daily in Asian songs and Caribbean food and folk studies meant to sustain the languages and cultures of a student body whose families came to Canada from Vietnam, China, the West Indies, and elsewhere. Their principal proudly announces that "diversity maintains a strength that can't be maintained if everything else is melted down."[9] But a research professor at the University of Ottawa finds that far from becoming balkanized, Canada's immigrants quickly absorb and accept Canada's basic liberal-democratic values, become citizens at rates higher than immigrants to the United States, learn English and French almost without exception, and partake of the general leavening of attitudes toward mixed marriages and other cultural issues.[10]

Another Toronto-based researcher goes even further. His research shows that it is rare for immigrant families to retain much of their native culture beyond the second generation. Shades of the Swedish and U.S. experience! Morton Weinfeld's history of Canadian multicultural policy was also discussed in chapter 9. That policy encourages diversity of culture in contrast to United States melting pot policies. In comparing the two countries with their contradictory policies,

Weinfeld found that assimilation occurs at the same rate in both.[11] Rodriguez's analysis of 1990 U.S. Census data reported the same three generational shift to English among both Latino and Asian immigrant families.[12] As this book nears its close, I wonder if Lipset chose to use the term "American Pluralism" in the title of his book on American assimilation because the word "assimilation" is (as Glazer suggested) dead or disreputable even though the phenomenon flourishes?[13]

Although language shift is an important indicator of assimilation, it is not the only one. Intermarriage also suggests that this process is occurring. The 1990 U.S. census data show that one-third of third generation Hispanic women marry non-Hispanics while 42 percent of third generation Asian women marry non-Asians. Demos describes how in the course of three or four generations, immigrant Greek women who live in Australia abandon demands that they marry only men from their ancestral Greek island. At first marriages to other Greek emigrants begin to occur. Eventually marriages to Australian men with no Greek ancestry become frequent. In three or four generations the community's Greek island heritage is evidenced only among the very old.[14] The same observation is made by Truehart in his analysis of Canadian immigrant policy: "the Canadian and American immigrant experience over the long haul, raise[s] the question: Is the mosaic ultimately a way station to the melting pot?"[15] This was of course the theoretical position of the Chicago School during the first half of the twentieth century. We will return to those Chicago sociologists shortly.

Further evidence of intermarriage is found in two studies conducted nearly a decade apart by Kennedy. She reports a clear trend toward intermarriage among ethnics in New Haven from 1870 to 1950. It is interesting that Kennedy does not find indiscriminate intermarriage. Ethnicity aside, religion erects barriers. Examining data on Catholic immigrants, she discovers that "Irish, Italians, and Poles intermarry mostly among themselves, and [among Protestants] British-Americans, Germans, and Scandinavians do likewise, while Jews seldom marry Gentiles."[16] Kennedy's Second World War-era observation on Jewish intermarriage is no longer true. Richardson reports that Jews are not only intermarrying at an accelerating pace but their parents are more accepting of this process according to 1990 surveys conducted by two Jewish organizations.[17]

No effort is made here to analyze the vast body of research dealing with ethnic and religious intermarriage. By and large the evidence is that it is widespread and increasing.[18] Recall that Australia, like Canada (although without its liberal immigration traditions), discovered that it was in its own interests to abandon its all-white immigration policy in 1972. It was replaced with a policy of "multiculturalism." Again, the consequences were the reverse of what was anticipated and intended. As Spurr put it: "Far from fighting to preserve their cultural identity, the ethnic rank and file was aggressively Australian and wanted to stay that way."[19]

What if we could experiment with a whole people and encourage half of them in their ethnicity while the other half was encouraged to assimilate? Such a natural experiment is approximated with the Azeri people. In the summer of 1993 Azerbaijan was losing a war with Armenia and was in a state of political chaos with its president having retreated from Baku to his home village, an acting president with no power or authority, and an entrepreneur with a private army apparently in control. Azerbaijanis are originally Iranian with some of their territory being ceded to Russia in 1828. It is reported that this national division did little to separate a people who were linguistically and culturally homogeneous. One observer argues that the Soviet policy of fostering Azeri nationalism, in contrast to the Iranian efforts to assimilate its Azeri minority, accounts for differences between the two Azeri groups. We are told by Hunter that "Many prominent Iranians are of Azerbaijani origins."[20] To the extent that this information is correct, the assimilated Azeri appear to have fared far better than their ethnically distinct brethren.

In chapter 3 we examined Peruvian policy as an instance which highlights the controversial nature of even benign efforts to promote the assimilation of indigenous peoples. In that chapter we described various instances of a "diversity policy" referred to as dumping and containing. Such policies are an outgrowth of slavery and forced labor and are viewed by some observers as a device which permits the dominant group to deal with its used up minorities in what appears to be a preservation effort. It raises the question: from whose perspective is the darkness of a policy defined? In this instance it seemed that the sympathetic protectors of the indigenous peoples would relegate them to reservations, referred to by some as "zoos" and others as "theme parks." This is truly an extreme diversity policy which intends to save an exotic culture and peoples. It may be that it is the preferred solution from the perspective of Amazon natives in Brazil or some American Indian groups. On the other hand, there are the young Peruvians who go to the city, adopt urban ways, and shift their identity from Indian to Mestizo. From their perspective an isolated reservation would be insufferable.

Assimilationist Policies: How and Why

The evidence to this point suggests that assimilation is a likely result of benignly administered pluralist or multicultural policies. Assimilationist policies are probably best implemented through initial pluralist policies. It is likely that many of the "quaint" and "picturesque" qualities of the minority are doomed with assimilation, although the kinds of ceremonial and sentimental survivals which Gans calls "symbolic ethnicity" may persist. This is precisely what is described in a study by Bakalian of Armenian Americans in New York and New Jersey. These people continue to take pride in their ethnic origins but "for most Armenian-Americans, Armenianness is food, hospitality, and generosity."[21] Much the same thing is found by Isajiwa and Podolosky among three generations of Germans, Italians, Jews, and Ukrainians in contemporary Toronto.[22] And in a comparative review of two American studies, Hirschman concludes that "Ethnicity did not determine one's career, marriage partner, friends, or neighborhood, but was an interesting extra to spice up life."[23]

But what of the revival of ethnic identity discussed in chapter 5? Glazer gives it short shrift: "We even had in the late 1960's and '70s, a brief explosion of revived ethnic assertiveness among white European ethnic groups. . . . It could not survive. Assimilation had gone too far."[24] There are scholars who would disagree with Glazer and they can rally considerable evidence to support their position. There is, as we saw in chapter 5, also evidence that there has been a revival of ethnic identity among Asian and Native Americans. As I pointed out in chapter 4, not all identities are ethnic and ethnic identities are not always the most salient ones in a person's notion of self.[25]

In the United States and among the descendants of European immigrants, considerable assimilation has occurred. The evidence above suggests that the same process is occurring among Latino and Asian immigrants. Ethnicity is indeed becoming largely symbolic. Is this a surprising phenomenon? It is not and I shall review below the theoretical literature which leads us to anticipate such a process. Is it desirable? I believe it is and I shall explain why below. But it is also true that there is a very dark side to assimilationist policies and it must be exposed and clarified so that well- intended policymakers do not inadvertently encourage it.

The Dark Side of Assimilation

I prefer a policy of high tolerance toward diversity to one of deliberate assimilation. The former seems to lead rapidly toward assimilation while the latter can have painful consequences for minorities. Examples of direct assimilationist policies in recent history are uniformly dark. Bulgaria's pre-1989 ethnic policy was aimed at Bulgarian Turks. Battiata tells us that under dictator Todor Zhivkov, they were compelled to "Bulgarize" their Islamic names and hundreds of thousands were forced to leave the country.[26] Romania, the only country where tanks and troops were used to resist the rebellion against the Soviet authorities, provides a particularly dramatic case. Ethnic Hungarians and Romanians joined together in Timisoara, the Transylvanian capital, to begin the overthrow of Nicolae Ceausescu. In 1988 Ceausescu had embarked on a deliberate policy of destroying all traces of Hungarian culture. Hungarian schools, radio stations, and newspapers were closed, the language was outlawed, and children could no longer be given Hungarian names—all in the name of national unity. According to McGrory, ethnic Hungarians saw the revolution as an opportunity to right old wrongs, but many Romanians saw it as a chance for their country to pull together.[27] For them the Hungarian demands for separate cultural institutions seemed divisive and unpatriotic. This is the essence of the difference between multiculturalists and assimilationists wherever they appear, including the United States and Canada. But in the Balkans, civil discourse is not the preferred method for solving intergroup differences.

Transylvania, where Hungarians and Romanians had united to rid themselves of the communist dictatorship, soon became a place of fears, tempers, and a violent nationalism. The worst violence in Romania's postwar history left at least three dead and hundreds injured.[28] McGrory believes that the only difference for Hungarians, Gypsies, and Germans who live in Romania is that now they have some possibility of achieving equality. Under Ceausescu the matter was not open to debate. Hungarians and Gypsies suffer a similar fate under the dark language laws of Slovakia, which impose the official language, both written and spoken, on all inhabitants. An observer in Slovakia writes that the language issue appears to be part of a strategy by Prime Minister Meciar to divide and conquer his political opponents.[29]

There is a dramatic moral contrast between the Swedish, Canadian, American, and Australian assimilationist policies and the brutal assimilationist policy aimed at Turks in Bulgaria or Hungarians in Romania, and the less brutal but equally discriminatory policy of the former ruling party on Taiwan. Sun writes that until recently children who spoke the native Taiwanese language in school were fined or punished and intermarriage between indigenous people and the descendants of the Chinese Nationalist invaders was frowned upon.[30] Suharto's policy toward ethnic Chinese in Indonesia[31] and that of the Beijing government toward the Muslim Uighrs in western China[32] mirror with precision the dark assimilationist policies of the Balkans. Language, traditions, schools, history, names—all are suppressed in the name of national unity. Indonesians compound such injustice by insisting that anyone with any Chinese ancestry, no matter how little and how far back, continues to be identified as Chinese. This dooms forever the assimilation which the Indonesian government claims to be the objective of its suppressive policies. Clearly, the conditions faced by ethnic Chinese in Indonesia are remarkably similar to those faced by African Americans.

The brighter side of assimilationist policy appears in the romantic image of the American melting pot, full of the varied spices of European immigrants eager to "Americanize." The reality of the American melting pot remains a hotly debated issue.[33] As effective as American assimilationist policy may have been with others, it has clearly failed with many native Americans and most African Americans. It is also true, as Glazer has observed, that American assimilation policy has fluctuated wildly between the benign notion of a melting pot and a dark concept of "Americanization" along with "un-American" attitudes and behaviors.[34] Nevertheless, all morally acceptable policies toward ethnic minorities must lie somewhere between the pluralist model of Ghana and the ultimately assimilationist model of Sweden.

Assimilation and Pluralism: The Logic of Evidence

Multicultural societies exist everywhere in time and place. They are clearly visible and there is an enormous literature describing and analyzing the relations among peoples who live in such societies. In contrast, assimilation, by definition is an invisible end product of intergroup relations. *One cannot study assimilated peoples since they are no longer there!* Where are the Norsemen in Normandy? Where are the Greeks in Sicily? Where are the Spaniards in Mexico? Where are the Saxons in Britain? (For that matter, where are the Normans?) These cases suggest that the assimilation of an ethnic group with others, rather than leading to the loss of a culture, results instead in the creation of peoples who are new and different from what had previously existed. When they assimilate, minorities do not disappear; they alter the cultural world of the dominant group.

It is little wonder that Lambert and Taylor's survey finds recent immigrants so opposed to assimilation. These investigators define assimilation, not as a blending, but as "the belief that cultural minorities should give up their so-called 'heritage' cultures and take on the 'American' way of life."[35] In the Western Hemisphere Wernet reminds us of the absorption of the Spanish invaders by the native peoples of Paraguay—a process not uncommon in Spanish and Portuguese America.[36]

In North America one thinks of the fate of native peoples in terms of segregation, isolation, even extermination, but rarely in assimilationist terms. It is, however, difficult to find a citizen of the western United States who does not claim some Indian ancestry and such citizens are not rare in the east. In part as a result of the census providing a choice of combination heritages for the first time, eastern states such as Maryland and Virginia tripled their Indian population in 2000 over what it was in 1990. In New Jersey the numbers doubled over the decade. In Oklahoma, the Cherokee tribe has more than doubled to 230,000 members over the past decade. According to Morello, from whose census data analysis these figures derive, "only those with an unbroken chain of family documents are enrolled [in the Cherokee tribe]."[37]

Nor was it unusual for American Negroes to engage in the practice of "passing" in order to evade the rampant prejudice and discrimination under Jim Crow that did not begin to dissipate until *Brown v. Board of Education* in 1954. According to Myrdal "'passing' is the backwash of miscegenation, and one of its surest results."[38] However, after reviewing research employing genealogical methods as well as various demographic techniques,[39] he was forced to conclude, as I have, that "It is difficult to determine the extent of passing [or assimilation in general]."[40]

Although there appears to have been little change in the amount of prejudice against African Americans in the United States, overt discrimination has steadily declined as a result of court rulings and civil rights legislation. Combined with a resurgent black pride, this may have resulted in a diminished rate of passing among light skinned African-Americans. As with any case of assimilation, the extent of the process must by definition remain mysterious.[41]

This discussion would be incomplete without the observation that assimilation is not the sole explanation for the disappearance of minorities. As I noted in chapter 3, annihilation of a minority can have the same result. According to Chandrasekaran, the original British settlers in Australia "regarded the Aborigines as little more than pests that needed to be driven away or killed." Apparently they were successful at least on the island of Tasmania where "colonists killed so many Aborigines that the indigenous population was wiped out by 1876."[42] Hitler's "final solution" almost eliminated Jews from Europe and American policy toward native peoples at times paralleled that of the Australians. Eventually both Australia and the United States resorted to reservations in barren parts of their respective continents as a means of isolating natives. Chandrasekaran describes the bizarre Australian government policy of kidnaping indigenous children for adoption by white families on the assumption that this would result in older natives eventually dying off and younger ones being assimilated. This persisted from the early 1900s into the mid-1970s, clearly a dark assimilation policy.

All of this said, where does it take us in terms of what is possible and what is desirable? I hold no quarrel with the idea of the melting pot; nor do I find anything horrifying in the concept of multiculturalism. I do not necessarily believe that the blending of peoples leads to a loss of their heritage and an increasing blandness of the society. Nor do I necessarily believe that cultural pluralism results in a polarized society divided by ethnic identities. On the other hand, my own values lead me to believe that certain end states are more desirable than others. I will close this book with a discussion of this value position. But first, let us consider why there is no surprise in finding extensive assimilation wherever in the world people are not maligned and mistreated because of their ethnic origins and sometimes even when they are so treated.

The Fit Between Theory and Data

One of the founders of American sociology, Robert E. Park, came to the discipline from a career as a journalist. He defined sociology as a quest for the "Big News." No matter how excellent the reporting of news, it is devoted to specific events in time. It is the job of sociology to find the relationships among events and to discover the processes which generate those relationships. Most of my evidence concerns only one nationality or one ethnic group or one religious conflict. This is true of both the scholarly literature and the articles available in the daily press. Taking my cue from Park, I am in search of the big news.

Articulating a theory of minority adaptation developed by Park and his colleagues at the University of Chicago early in this century, Louis Wirth insists that "pluralistic minorities . . . are merely way stations on the road to other stages." Furthermore, "The possibility of the ultimate assimilability of ethnic groups is thus beyond doubt."[43] This was advanced by the Chicago people as an inevitable process. As difficult as it is to swallow such deterministic imagery with its fuzzy time limits, we have seen that there is considerable evidence that it does happen—at least in some places, under some conditions, and with some minorities. Park and Miller argued that a wise policy of assimilation, like a wise educational policy, does not seek to destroy the attitudes and memories that are there, but to build on them."[44] They might well have been advisers to the architects of the Swedish home language education policy. Why, then, should one be surprised by this evidence?

Working with statements by Park such as, "It is participation rather than submission or conformity that makes Americans of foreign born peoples,"[45] Lal concludes that the Chicago school's writing on immigrants, "may be read as an effort to explain their paradoxical observation that participation in separate immigrant institutions facilitated acculturation and the immigrant's participation in the institutions of the wider American community."[46] The Chicago theory suggests that pluralist policy has assimilationist consequences. This is a theme which we have found confirmed in a variety of evidence drawn from contemporary minority policies—Australia, Canada, Sweden, and the United States, for example. It is also a theme which dominated American sociological thinking on minority group processes for nearly half a century until fashions in such thinking began to change during the 1960s. Within that theoretical framework the evidence reviewed in this chapter is precisely what would be expected. Again, the evidence is not surprising. It is simply confirmatory.

The contemporary world is in constant flux—evolving (or devolving) from day to day into something different. One of the first signs of the hysteria in America following the September 2001 destruction of the World Trade Towers in New York City was the repetitious pronouncement by press and politicians that the world would never be the same after that day. That is correct. But it was just as correct the day before and the day after. The world changes every day. In the empirical world it would be difficult to identify a truly assimilationist or a truly pluralist society. The concepts of assimilation and pluralism are useful imaginary types which can be constructed in something approximating their pure imagined form. As Wirth observed, "We should not expect to find . . . these types to occur in pure form either in history or in the present."[47] Such constructs, called "Ideal Types" by Max Weber, provide the poles which set standards for judging the reality which appears between them.[48] Although we may speak of peoples as "assimilated" or "pluralist," it is always a matter of more or less. Consider the following example.

In an analysis based largely on personal interviews and U.S. Census data, Garreau found it odd that Washington, D.C., has no Koreatown. The great American urban ghettos of the nineteenth and early twentieth centuries, populated by Chinese, Italians, Irish, Jews, Poles, etc., are familiar to all Americans, most of whose ancestors lived in such places. As we enter the twenty-first century new ethnic enclaves continue to be established. In Washington, for example, they are created by Salvadorans, Ethiopians, and Vietnamese. Although these are relatively small, large enclaves do continue to come into being. Witness the Arab suburb of Dearborn just outside of Detroit.

Most Koreans live in the Washington suburbs and in the most heavily populated Korean neighborhood, only one household in twelve is Korean.[49] The major differences between these people and the nineteenth-century immigrants, according to Hyung Chan Kim,[50] is that the Koreans are urban, educated, citizens of the modern world. In these respects the Korean immigrant is as much at home in Washington, D.C., as in Seoul. Not only are the immigrants different, but contemporary America is different. Illsoo Kim observes that, among other changes, "civil rights and anti-discrimination policies have limited the most manifest discrimination against all ethnic and racial minorities."

Garreau believes that all of this lessened any inclination to cluster into tight geographic knots with other people from Korea. His informants say things like, "My people want to get into the main stream," or "We are not going to go to a neighborhood because there are many Korean guys." Both Kims and Garreau appear to agree that the key to the dispersion of Korean immigrants lies in the high value they place on education and that value has been documented by Underwood.[51] Their prime criteria in deciding where to live is the quality of the public schools. "You shop for the school district. Education is the number one priority." McGee[52] points out that, thanks to changing times and laws, new immigrants are free to live wherever they can afford. In the nineteenth century restrictive covenants and antiforeigner sentiment limited the residential choices for immigrants. For most of the Italians, Irish, Jews, and Poles, the slums provided the only affordable housing. Education and income are also different. If the old wave of immigrants were mostly poor and uneducated, the new wave of Asians finds a ready market demanding their professional and high-tech positions.

If we were limited to this much information, it would be necessary to conclude that Korean immigrants are rapidly assimilating into American society. But there is more. Garreau writes of "office condominiums full of Korean attorneys, accountants and associations." As it turns out, his "assimilated" Koreans associate almost exclusively with other Koreans both on an informal personal basis and on a business basis. Furthermore, the family shopping and religious associations are also exclusively Korean. In spite of residential integration and the absorption of American values, Koreans appear to retain ethnic associations and institutions. They are neither assimilated nor pluralist. Rather, they fall somewhere in between. The Chicago sociologists would see them as in the process of becoming assimilated. The reader of this book would simply shrug and say, "Wait for the third generation."

Recent Korean immigrants are not unique in exhibiting this mixture of assimilation and pluralism as they find their way in the new society. At the turn of the last century, other ethnic groups preceded them along the same path. In a story on the history of the Jewish Community Center in Washington, D.C., which opened in 1926, Meyer writes that "long before multiculturalism came into vogue and at a time when immigrants wanted to escape rather than cling to their roots, the JCC proudly promoted 'Americanism.'"[53] I suspect I was not the only small child in Brooklyn in the 1920s, to hear foreigners belittled by a chauvinist immigrant grandfather. People who did not speak English, he said in his heavy accent, were un-American. I am told that contemporary Korean immigrants are shifting rapidly to English and that in Chicago they openly opposed bilingual education.

These people, whether Koreans in the 1990s or Jews in the 1920s, are involved in a process which Park regards as en route toward assimilation.[54] Following Park's lead, the Chicago school viewed assimilation as the end result of a process through which all immigrants needed to go. Their thesis was indeed a safe one, since they put no time limit on the process, making it impossible to disprove it. Nevertheless, the Korean anecdote illuminates the complexity of such a process. It must be in a state of continual flux and there is no point at which an identifiable ethnic group can be described as fully assimilated or fully pluralistic. In chapter 14 we consider the notions of "assimilation" and "pluralism" in light of a world embarking on the twenty-first century. Is one of these processes "better" than the other? If so, which one? And, finally, why is it better?

Notes

1.*White Teeth* is in truth not the "African-American slave saga." In fact it is an earthy saga of a Bangladeshi family and a Jamaican-Cockney family and their lifelong multigenerational friendship in a working-class London neighborhood. These are black, brown, and white people for whom color seems very low on the hierarchy of important things. The quote is from Esther Iverem, "London Calling," a review of Zadie Smith, *White Teeth* in *Book World, Washington Post,* 21 May 2000, 7. The book is *White Teeth* (New York: Random House, 2000).

2. Adam Podgorecki, "Sociotechnics: Basic Concepts and Issues" in *Dilemmas of Effective Social Action*, ed. Jerzy Kubin (Warsaw: Polish Sociological Association, 1990), 19-40.

3. R. Herrnstein and C. Murray, *The Bell Curve* (New York: Free Press, 1994).

4. Ashley Montagu, *Man's Most Dangerous Myth: The Fallacy of Race* (Walnut Creek, Calif.: Altamira Press, 1997).

5. Nathan Glazer, *We Are All Multiculturalists Now* (Cambridge, Mass.: Harvard University Press, 1997), 119.

6. Richard D. Alba and Victor Nee, "Rethinking Assimilation Theory for a New Era of Immigration," *International Migration Review* 31 (winter 1997): 826-74.

7. K. Hyltenstam and L. Arnberg, "Bilingualism and Education of Immigrant Children

and Adults in Sweden," in *International Handbook of Bilingualism and Bilingual Education,* ed. Christine Paulston (New York: Greenwood Press: New York, 1988).

8. *Time,* 22 December 1992. The article reports that the research was done by Rodolfo O. de la Garza, University of Texas-Austin. I have been chided for employing secondary data found in newspaper reports rather than tracking down original sources. My defense of this practice appears in chapter six.

9. Howard Schneider, "Canada: A Mosaic, Not a Melting Pot," *Washington Post,* 5 July 1998, 15(A).

10. I have carelessly misplaced the source of this lucid statement and regret being unable to attribute it properly. It further confirms Canadian findings reported here by Turehart, Schneider, and Weinfeld.

11. Morton Weinfeld, "Canadian Jews and Canadian Pluralism," in *American Pluralism and the Jewish Community,* ed., Seymour Martin Lipset (New Brunswick, N.J.: Transaction Publishers, 1990), 87-106.

12. Gregory Rodriguez, "It Only Takes a Generation or Three," *Washington Post,* 4 July 1999, 3(B).

13. Seymour Martin Lipset, ed., *American Pluralism and the Jewish Community* (New Brunswick, N.J.: Transaction Publishers, 1990).

14. Vasilikie Demos, "The Production of Ethnicity among Greek Kytherian Women in Australia" (paper presented at the annual meeting of the North Central Sociological Association, Fort Wayne, Indiana, April 1992).

15. Charles Truehart, "O Canada! . . . Whose Canada?" *Washington Post,* 5 May 1996, 1(A) and 27(A).

16. The two studies by Ruby Jo Reeves Kennedy are, "Single or Triple Melting Pot? Intermarriage in New Haven, 1870-1940," *American Journal of Sociology* 49 (January 1944): 331-39 and "Single or Triple Melting Pot? Intermarriage in New Haven, 1870-1950," *American Journal of Sociology* 58 (July 1952): 56-59.

17. Lynda Richardson, "Jews Accepting Intermarriage, Survey Says," *Washington Post,* 18 September 1990.

18. Further evidence appears in a paper on Irish Americans by Hout and one on Hawaiians by Labov and Jacobs. See Michael Hout, "Living With diversity: Irish Intermarriage in the United States" (paper presented at the annual meetings of the American Sociological Association. Cincinnati, Ohio, 26 August 1991) and Teresa Labov and Jerry A. Jacobs, "Trends in Intermarriage and Interracial Births in Hawaii: Adjusting for Multiple Ancestry" (paper presented at the annual meetings of The American Sociological Association. Cincinnati, Ohio, 25 August 1991).

19. Russell Spurr, "Australia Goes Asian," *New York Times Magazine* (4 December 1998): 46-49, 52 and 56.

20. Shireen T Hunter, *Washington Post,* 21 January 1990.

21. Anny Bakalian, "From Being to Feeling Armenian: Assimilation and Identity Among Armenian Americans" (paper presented at the annual meetings of the American Sociological Association. Cincinnati, Ohio, August 1991).

22. Wesvold W. Isajiwa and Momo Podolosky, "The Deconstruction and Reconstruction of Ethnicity in Culturally Diverse Societies" (paper presented at the annual meeting of The American Sociological Association. Cincinnati, Ohio, August 1991).

23. Charles Hirschman, "What Happened to the White Ethnics?" *Contemporary Sociology* 20 (March 1991):180-83. The two studies are Richard D. Alba, *Ethnic Identity: The Transformation of White America* (New Haven, Conn.: Yale University Press, 1990)

and Mary C. Waters, *Ethnic Options: Choosing Identities in America* (Berkeley: University of California Press, 1990).

24. Glazer, *We Are All Multiculturalists Now*, 118.

25. See Michael Banton and Mohd Noor Mansor, "The Study of Ethnic Alignment: A New Technique and an Application in Malaysia," *Ethnic and Racial Studies* 15, no. 4, (October 1992): 600-13.

26. Mary Battiata, *Washington Post*, 28 March 1990.

27. Mary McGrory, *Washington Post*, 13 March 1990.

28. This violence is, of course, minuscule compared to what was later to be perpetrated under the name of ethnic cleansing by Serbs and Croats against each other and the nominal Muslim peoples of the former Yugoslavia. See James Rupert, "Diplomats on Lonely Mission to Ease Tension in Yugoslav Regions," *Washington Post*, 9 June 1993, 28(A).

29. Christine Spolar, "Slovak Leader Fans Bias toward Hungarian Minority," *Washington Post*, 30 November 1997, 23(A).

30. Leona H. Sun, "Taiwan Election May Reflect Emerging Pride of a People," *Washington Post*, 21 December 1991.

31. Cindy Shiner, "For Indonesia's Ethnic Chinese, A New Era Revives Old Hatreds," *Washington Post*, 16 June 1988, 23-24(A).

32. Steven Mufson, "Ethnic Turmoil Roils Western China," *Washington Post*, 23 February 1997, 25(A).

33. An example of the heat generated by this issue can be found in the angry response by Greeley to Hirschman's sympathetic review of recent research supporting the American assimilationist position. See chap. 4, pp. 48-49.

34. Glazer, *We Are All Multiculturalists* Now, 108-109.

35. Walace E. Lambert and Donald M. Taylor, "Assimilation versus Multiculturalism: the Views of Urban Americans," *Sociological Forum* 3, no.1 (winter 1988).

36. Christine Wernet, "Ethnic Pluralism in Paraguay" (paper presented at the annual meetings of the Society for Applied Sociology, Cincinnati, Ohio, November, 1990). There is a certain irony, as Wernet notes, to the fact that a couple of centuries after absorbing their conquerors, the Paraguayans found themselves a "settler society" when an invited colony of German immigrants assumed political and economic control of the country.

37. Carol Morello, "Native American Roots, Once Hidden, Now Embraced," *Washington Post*, 7 April 2001, 1(A) and 12(A). The work of Joane Nagel is informative on this issue. See chapter 5, pp. 62-63. See Nagel's "American Indian Ethnic Renewal: Politics and the Resurgence of Identity," *American Sociological Review* 60 (December 1995): 947-65, and "Constructing Ethnicity: Creating and Recreating Ethnic Identity and Culture," *Social Problems* 41 (February 1994): 152-75.

38. Gunnar Myrdal with the assistance of Richard Sterner and Arnold Rose, *An American Dilemma: The Negro Problem and Modern Democracy* (New York: Harper & Brothers, 1944), 129.

39. Myrdal, *An American Dilemma*, n49, 207-208.

40. Myrdal, *An American Dilemma*, 129.

41. For a contemporary and very personal analysis of the process of "passing" and its consequences see Shirlee Haizlip, *The Sweeter the Juice: A Family Memoir in Black and White* (New York: Simon and Schuster,1997).

42. Rajiv Chandrasekaran, *Washington Post*, 6 July 2000, 1(A) and 17(A).

43. Louis Wirth, "The Problem of Minority Groups," in *Louis Wirth on Cities and Social Life,* ed. Albert J. Reiss, Jr. (Chicago, Ill.: The University of Chicago Press, 1964),

256, 269.

44. Robert E. Park and Herbert A. Miller, *Old World Traits Transplanted* (New York: Harper and Brothers., 1921, 280.

45. Robert E. Park, *The Immigrant Press and Its Control* (New York: Harper and Brothers, 1922), 88.

46. Barbara Ballis Lal, "Perspectives on Ethnicity: Old Wine in New Bottles," *Ethnic and Racial Studies* 6, no. 2 (April 1983.): 159-60.

47. Wirth, "The Problem of Minority Groups," 245.

48. For an example of Weber's application of the concept to "Capitalism," see Hans H. Gerth and C. Wright Mills, translators and editors, *From Max Weber: Essays in Sociology* (New York: Oxford University Press, 1946), 265-69.

49. Joel Garreau, "Area Koreans See No Need for Enclaves," *Washington Post*, 11 January 1992, 1(E) and 9(E).

50. Quotations and references to Hyung Chan Kim and Illsoo Kim are from interviews reported by Garreau and not to their books. See Hyung Chan Kim, *The Korean Diaspora* (London: Clio Press, 1977) and Ilsoo Kim, *New Urban Immigrants* (Princeton, N.J.: Princeton University Press, 1981).

51. Horace Underwood, *The Korean Way* (Seoul: Christian Literature Society of Korea, 1977).

52. Reece McGee in a personal communication, March 2001.

53. Eugene L. Meyer, "The Center of Their Lives," *Washington Post*, 20 January 1992.

54. Robert E. Park, "Our Racial Frontiers on the Pacific," *Survey Graphic*, 56, no. 3 (11 May 1926): 192-96.

Chapter 14

The End: Values, Politics, and Assimilation

In the 1930s I think the popularity of people like Jack Benny and Groucho Marx made the whole country a little bit Jewish. And I think that jazz certainly makes the whole country more than a little bit African American.

—Garry Giddins, "Critic" on the television production *Jazz*, January 2001

Where does all of this leave us? Clearly, the world suffers from the vestigial remains of European colonialism. It is the universal appendix and is prone to periodic bursting. The potential for racial and ethnic violence lurks everywhere. It is nearly always masked in the righteous justification of religion: Christian crusaders, Hindu fanatics, Jewish extremists, and Muslim terrorists all claim divine sanction for their willingness to give their lives in opposing the right of "the other" to exist. All are convinced that the gods are on their side. I use the term "masked" advisedly, since there is nearly always present a blend of class distinctions with their mix of privilege and deprivation along with some real or mythical ancient score to be settled.

Three examples dating well before the colonial era will suffice. Orthodox Serbs and Catholic Croats continue to nurse a 500-year-old grudge against their Muslim cousins. Their grudge against each other extends even further—well over a millennium. Irish Catholics and Protestants are more recent, with their animosity dating a mere 400 years into the past.[1] The hostility between Hindu and Muslim extremists in India dates back to the medieval Mogul conquest and cannot be completely blamed upon the British. It seems always to be the poorest masses of a society who are most easily mobilized to take to the barricades against their neighbors.

A leading sociologist of religion pointed out to me that I was being unjustly harsh on religion which she believes has done more good than harm. Paloma observed that people who intend harm to other people will always find some excuse or justification for their evil deeds. If not religion, than something else.[2]

Reflecting on this, it occurred to me that neither Hitler nor Stalin required religious justification for the terrors they committed. The Khmer Rouge, who slaughtered much of their own population is a more recent secular example. In part 2 we examined five treatments or preventions for the problem. All have been successful for periods of time under certain conditions. The world needs to take account of the enclave solution embraced by Ghana's Chieftaincy Act and the effective integration of peoples of diverse nationalities and cultures achieved by the Swedish educational policies of the mid-1970s. Those same Swedish policies deal effectively with problems posed to a nation by foreign sojourners. The world is familiar with the partition solution and, in spite of its sometimes dark side, its relative costs and benefits are in need of reassessment. South Africa's effort to renounce vengeance with its Truth and Reconciliation Commission was widely publicized and in all probability helped to prevent massive bloodshed after the fall of the European autocracy in that nation. What is less widely recognized is the success of similar policies in several South America nations as well as elsewhere in the world. Ruminating on the evidence reviewed in this book led me to a reconsideration of the allegedly outdated and sometimes maligned concept of "assimilation."

We have seen that the term "assimilation" suffers from poor popular repute. Let us pursue the values and the politics of the assimilationist policies implied by the data presented in chapter 13. At the end of the Second World War, Wirth, one of the last survivors of the Chicago School, acknowledged the short run persistence of ethnic, linguistic, and religious divisions, but he had great faith in what he saw as an increasing secular trend in the modern world, "which manifests itself in the spread of rationalism, science, and the general skepticism toward ideas and beliefs inherited from the past."[3] He believed that the spread of democracy would put an end to ethnic squabbling and hatreds. In his optimistic postwar view, Wirth also believed that "a 'holy war' is almost inconceivable in modern times." The term has been commonplace since the September 11, 2001, attack on the United States by Islamic extremists. He did not live long enough to see the nationalist and ethnic shambles democratization brought with it to Eastern Europe, the Balkans, and much of the former Soviet Union. Nor did he foresee the political wreckage left of much of Africa with the end of the cold war. He could not have anticipated the hatred of Muslim extremists toward the United States or the deadly holy war between Palestinians and Israelis.

Wirth was not the only leading authority whose crystal ball betrayed him. Ashley Montagu was a contemporary of Wirth's. Montagu's classic history, critique, and analysis of the idea of race failed to foresee, and does not incorporate in later editions, the new wave of racial and ethnic pride which has swept the United States along with its consequences for ethnicity. This movement has stood on its head some of the arguments concerning the evils of the idea of race which Montagu equates with "caste"and which he hopes will be replaced by ethnicity.[4] It is not my intention to disparage the genius of either Wirth or

Montagu. The flaw is found not in their scholarship but in the unpredictability of history itself. The world is not the same.

As we move into the twenty-first century, there is nothing "inconceivable" about the idea of a holy war among many Muslims, Jews, Christians, and Hindus. Religious fanatics wield considerable political influence in the United States, Northern Ireland, Israel, Serbia, Pakistan, India, Iran, probably Afghanistan, and at least a half-dozen African nations (to mention only a few places). In a world where the leaders of the most powerful nation persist in urging the populace to solve problems by praying, and where creationism achieves parity with evolution, Wirth's image of a secular, rational, scientific world reflects little more than the optimism of the immediate postwar era.

In his first and somewhat belated statement following the destruction of the twin towers in Manhattan and the attack on the pentagon, President George W. Bush announced that we would get even and we should all pray.[5] I found this approach to problem solving neither comforting nor constructive. The reverends Jerry Falwell and Pat Robertson jointly informed the world that those destructive acts were God's way of suggesting that we had all gone astray in our indulgence in evils such as abortion, homosexuality, feminism, adultery, supporting the American Civil Liberties Union, and other unnatural abominations.[6]

What Robertson describes defensively as "a theological discussion" is reported by Harris in the *Washington Post* and Goodstein in the *New York Times*.[7] Apparently God had gotten even. This is not too surprising since the religious fanatics who had murdered thousands of unsuspecting civilians in less than an hour had done so in the name of the same God. Meanwhile some patriotic Americans set about beating and murdering other Americans who they thought might be Muslims.[8]

The message (back in chapter 1) of the two Hungarians in Ottawa was that this new awakening of religion does not bode well for minority groups. In fact, when it is the minority which displays religious fanaticism and intolerance, it does not bode well for the dominant group either. Bloom describes the relationship between members of an extreme Jewish sect and their tolerant small town Midwestern American hosts.[9] The sect operates a local slaughter house with the aim of providing kosher meat for their fellow Lubavich Hassidim elsewhere in the United States. A Lubovich interviewed by Bloom provides a lucid expression of the identity of all ethnic extremists who simultaneously resist assimilation and despise diversity. It is the epitome of intolerance for those who are "different": "Wherever we go, we don't adapt to the place or the people. It's the place and people who have to adapt to us." This is a policy adopted by world leaders ranging from Attila the Hun to Adolph Hitler. According to one reviewer, the Hassidim offered the author what he calls "a view of the dark side of my own faith, a look at Jewish extremists who not only made the [locals] wince, but made me wince too."[10] How often does the definition of one's own group as "different" become a definition of one's own group as "superior"?

The concept of "ideal types" in Max Weber's detached sense of constructed polar opposites is incomplete in describing the notions of pluralism and assimilation. They are also ideals in the valuational sense of the word. The remainder of this chapter focuses on that ideological diversion. Multiculturalists believe that pluralism is not only good, but that it also leads to a better society. An example is provided by Monique Deveaux's defense of diversity as just, moral, and to the ultimate benefit of all parties.[11] In contrast, the Chicago people believed that assimilation was not only good, but it leads to a better society. Curiously, both groups agree that the short run and the long run are different and that there is a certain inevitability to assimilation in the long run—however long that may be. As we have seen, there is evidence to support that conclusion.

Ethnic history in America over the past few decades is relevant here and in spite of Glazer's short shrift,[12] I believe it has important consequences. I have dealt with that history in chapters 4 and 5 but a few reminders may be helpful. Recall that there was considerable confusion in the supposedly neat dichotomies of liberal-conservative and pluralist-assimilationist. Matters appeared messy in this regard. Let us reconsider Waxman's partial reconciliation of some of the contradictions. He struggled with the confrontation of his pluralist aspirations by the hard empirical data he encountered. Ultimately he acknowledged that he is an ideological pluralist, but he conceded reluctantly that he is also an empirical assimilationist: "the empirical assimilationist is one who, regardless of his own personal ideology and hopes, foresees, on the basis of his interpretation of the empirical evidence, the ultimate assimilation of large segments of the American Jewish population."[13]

My argument is not limited to that particular ethnic group; it is a universal one. The evidence allows only for Waxman's choice. I too must be an empirical assimilationist. But, unlike Waxman, I choose also to be an ideological assimilationist. That choice requires explanation and justification. It is true as I informed my doubting Indian students that a deliberate assimilationist policy is no longer fashionable in the United States or in Canada. Is it then fair to conclude that policies designed to facilitate assimilation are neither desirable nor possible? Such a conclusion may be justified at least in part by some of the darker assimilationist policies mentioned in chapter 13.

On the other hand, we have seen evidence that policies which are designed to provide for a multicultural society do in fact lead to assimilation. Furthermore, there was evidence that, left to their own devices, ethnics gradually assimilate or at least divorce themselves from their original ethnic culture. Demos's research, which was reviewed in chapter 13, documents this process among immigrant Australian women from a Greek island.[14] Much the same process has been observed among other Australian minorities as well as Canadians, Swedes, and Americans.

We have seen confirmation of the argument of the Chicago sociologists early in this century that the process of assimilation, if not inevitable, is nearly as

difficult to turn back as the tides. That is the empirical side. What of the ideology? Why do I find myself sharing the unfulfilled optimism of Park and Wirth?
When arrived at by benign policies, I suspect that assimilation is desirable in
terms of social cohesion and social solidarity and the reduction of intergroup
conflict. To extend the definition of a human being—someone not different from
one's self—beyond the family, beyond the tribe, beyond the village, beyond the
nation, and perhaps eventually to include all of the world's humanity is to make
xenophobia meaningless.

In the nineties a body of literature began to emerge and with it the now
common term, "rescuers." Although it confirms the dark intergroup picture
painted above, it also suggests more optimistic possibilities. That literature takes
as its point of departure the concept of "extensivity" developed by Samuel and
Pearl Oliner in their study of European gentiles who had risked their lives to
rescue Jews from the Nazis.[15]

The Oliners found no difference between their rescuers and a control group
in various personality factors, in the extent to which they were outsiders or more
adventurous or more religious or even in the extent to which they were anti-Nazi.
What they did find was that the rescuers were more empathic—more easily
moved by pain than the control group. Furthermore, they discovered that these
empathic rescuers had been raised in families where they had been witness to
compassionate behavior—in contrast to talk. The fragility of the linkage between
what people say and what they otherwise do has been well documented.[16]

For the Oliners, extensivity is the essence of the altruistic personality. It has
to do with "how far out from your own family or group you extend your compassion and concern. The rescuers, it turned out, didn't care only for people like
themselves. The 'Us' vs. 'Them' impulse was weak in them."[17] That personality
trait, to be useful in thinking about national policies, must be converted into a
social concept. A sociological hypothesis based upon it would go something like:
The more the in-group boundaries extend from the family to the world at large,
the less likely people are collectively to do damage to one another.

A temporarily successful effort to achieve a degree of extensivity can be
found in the pan-Yugoslav policies of Tito. Rescuers exist under the worst of
conditions although stories of them do not make such dramatic news as the tales
of hate and destruction which are so common. Although small attention was paid,
Williams has told tales of Serb and Muslim neighbors in Kosovo who watched
over each others property after one or the other had fled and saw that it was
safely returned when the refugees came home.[18]

A precursor to the Oliners' policy-oriented work was provided by Milgram's
laboratory research on conformity.[19] This and related work graphically documented the manner in which most people would behave in ways expected of them
by others—especially when those others were in a position of authority. Even
though research subjects often expressed sentiments to the contrary, they would
nevertheless continue to inflict pain upon other people when it was expected of

them. Although the thrust of this and related research was to document the extent to which people behave as they are expected to, regardless of any inner convictions, it is noteworthy that substantial minorities consistently refused to cooperate with the experimenter in injuring the experimental subject. I have reviewed and analyzed these data elsewhere.[20]

As with the Oliners' more recent work, the experimental literature on conformity finds no association between conforming behavior and any specific personality or demographic characteristics. All kinds of people do what everyone else is doing and what seems to be expected of them. The Oliners attribute the difference between rescuers and others to the child's observation of parental behaviors. I toyed with David Riesman's rich distinction between "Other-directed" and "Inner-directed" social types.[21] Inner-directed types, unlike other-directed ones, would more likely make behavioral decisions based on certain inner convictions. In dealing with this social psychological literature it is imperative to avoid involvement in a morass of individual motivation. We are, after all, dealing with mass movements involving socially and culturally defined groups and with national policies related to such mass intergroup behavior. Nevertheless, useful clues to understanding our problem may be found in this literature.

As we learn in anthropology 101, the languages of some isolated tribal peoples both in the Americas and in Africa reserve the word "human being" for members of their own tribe. Other peoples are not human and are not treated as such. The term "peoplehood" is sometimes used in contemporary efforts to understand national identities.[22] Consider the semantics of that term! Are the implications much different from those tribal usages of "human beings"? More direct is the ancient Jewish concept of chosenness: "The word 'chosen' is used sparingly in the bible. . . . It's antonym is not 'considered impartially' or 'ignored,' but 'despised.'"[23] Couple this definition with Hertzberg's observation that "the essence of Judaism is the affirmation that the Jews are the chosen people: all else is commentary."[24] Such notions must be disquieting to outsiders. They are of course not peculiar to Jews. The idea of one's own people being the chosen of God is universal among Christians and Muslims. Romani Gypsies have a vocabulary for it and one of the three bases for anti-Catholicism in Northern Ireland is what Brewer calls the "covenantal mode" which emphasizes Protestants as the chosen people and Catholics as the enemy.[25]

Writing of the deadly targeting of children because of their ethnic identity in Northern Ireland, Kigali, Srebrenica, and elsewhere, Meg Greenfield describes how the self-styled chosen ones are able to dehumanize others as nonpeople— the predator's perception of the prey:

> What we are seeing here . . . is the blotting out of both the assailant's and the target's identity and individuality and very humanity. All that matters in ethnic wars is the ethnic extraction of the victim. You are not killing actual human beings. You are cleaning out pests.[26]

The goal of Pol Pot was the conquest of Vietnam in order to exterminate all *yuon*—a pejorative term for Vietnamese which roughly translates as "barbarians." According to a May 1978 Khmer Rouge radio broadcast, "In terms of numbers one of us must kill 30 Vietnamese [in order to annihilate them]."[27] Is it necessary to remind the reader of the Nazi distinction between Aryans and *untermensch*—Jews, Poles, Gypsies, Slavs, and all brown and black people?

To those who claim that we ought to take pride in our ethnic heritage, *I submit that pride of ancestry is false pride which reflects no accomplishments of one's self—only those of others, and if we take pride in the accomplishments of ancestors do we accept blame for the harm they may have done to others?* My values suggest that we deserve neither credit nor blame.

In the nations of the world at the turn of the twenty-first century, the "others" may be slaughtered as essentially nonhumans or they may be treated with a patronizing tolerance, or, as is probably more often the case, the relationship falls somewhere between these extremes. It seems paradoxical that in order to fully realize ourselves as social creatures who thrive on a group identity, we must despise and, to some degree, ultimately mistreat other social creatures. As long as there is a "we" and a "they," we will ultimately perceive ourselves as superior and perceive them as inferior.

Is there a solution to such an unsavory paradox? There is nothing inherently human in the notion of chosen people which excludes all others. Language expressing this imagery can disappear. And with it will disappear the infidel, the *goyem*, the heathen, the *gadze*, the pagan, and other expressions of contempt for those who are thought to be different. It seems to me that this is desirable. As I moved toward these conclusions after a decade of work, I was at first troubled by the politics of some of my tentative conclusions. The evidence suggests clearly that when immigrant minorities and their cultures are treated with respect, they become smoothly absorbed into the dominant society in about three generations. This diminishes the we-they distinctions. In doing so, it also diminishes some of the diversity in society. I approve of that.

But I remain uneasy about a politics of assimilation, not only because of its dark side but also because it places me in the company of a frightening assembly of people who are often contemptuous of cultures and languages and religions other than their own. These are the people who spit out terms like "politically correct" when confronting someone with a different view in these matters. I am not alone in this failure to find a comfortable political niche. In Michael Fletcher's interview with the authors of a controversial book on affirmative action he discovers that they consider themselves to be 1950s style liberals but find themselves on the cutting edge of contemporary conservatism.[28] Like those authors, I prefer to distance myself and my position from that of the cultural and linguistic and religious chauvinists whose ethnocentrism causes such pain to so many people in the world.[29] The fact that multicultural policies benignly administered can lead quickly to assimilation is one way to accomplish that. It suggests that multicultural policies are the best place to begin.

The comment by Garry Giddins which opens this chapter suggests a second argument which distances my position from that of the conservatives. It is the recognition that assimilation is a two-way street which may benefit or injure both the dominant and the minority group. Just as Swedish society has been enriched by its immigrant influence, so too has the Dutch. The blending of ways by the cool Dutch and the warm Surinamese is remarkable. Robinsons's interviews dramatically document this. On the one hand, a Surinamer tells him, "You have to change. The situation brings change. Here you don't have time for friends and they don't have time for you. When you want to visit friends, you have to phone first and make an appointment. . . . After six o'clock you cannot visit people in Holland. Everyone is inside. People live inside." Surinam immigrants must change, but so too must the Dutch! Another immigrant interviewed by Robinson spins this telling tale:

> A few years ago I was at *Leidseplein* waiting for the tram, going home at night. I looked around and it hit me: when I came over here, when I would be going out at 12 at night with my Surinamese friends, the Dutch were all going home. But here I was, on my way home, and all around me were these Dutch people going out. They were wearing beautiful clothes, beautiful shoes, they were using their hands when they talked, gesturing the way we might.[30]

This immigrant has observed a profound change in the host society. They have become more like him! Murray Wax reminds us that it is not only European culture and it is not only the quaint and the colorful that is absorbed: "Our number system derives from India; our alphabet from the Middle East. A significant plurality of our vegetables and crops derives from the native peoples of the Americas."[31] The third argument for distancing my position from the conservatives lies in the general state of confusion and flux. As we saw in chapter 13, there is no distinct right- or left-wing position in these matters. Then what is there for me to distance myself from?

This story has a happy ending. There are conditions under which national policies have facilitated a congenial relationship between minority and dominant groups. Sometimes the solution is as simple as partition as with the Czechs and Slovaks. Unquestionably, the rejection of vengeance reduces dangers in the transition from an oppressive regime to a more democratic one as in South Africa. When people seem unwilling or unable to get along, the Ghanaian Chieftaincy Act provides a model for a peaceful solution, one which may suit some in the Balkans as well as in other tribal societies such as Afghanistan.

Most hopeful is the finding that encouraging diversity leads eventually to assimilation. The second generation becomes an integral part of the larger society and the grandchildren will believe that what it is all about is good food, good music, special holidays, and colorful costumes. Who can argue with that? Well, perhaps Adolph Hitler, Joseph Stalin, Patrice Lumumba, Slobodan Milosevic, the Ayatollah Khomeini, and Jerry Falwell. This book began with the well chosen words of Shylock, but Rodney King is more succinct: "We are all stuck here for a while. Let's try to work it out." (in a public appeal for calm uttered in Los Angeles on May 1, 1992).

Notes

1. A contemporary analysis of one of these histories can be found in John D. Brewer (with Gareth I. Higgins), *Anti-Catholicism in Northern Ireland, 1600-1998: The Mote and the Beam* (New York: St. Martin's Press, 1998).

2. This is a loosely paraphrased recollection of a conversation with Margaret Paloma.

3. Louis Wirth, "The Problem of Minority Groups," in *Louis Wirth on Cities and Social Life*, ed. A. J. Reiss, Jr. (Chicago: University of Chicago Press, 1964), 264.

4. Ashley Montagu, *Man's Most Dangerous Myth: The Fallacy of Race* (Walnut Creek, Calif.: Altamira Press, 1997), 180 and elsewhere.

5. Radio and Television address, 11 September 2001.

6. Televised discussion on "The 700 Club," 12 September 2001.

7. Laurie Goodstein, *New York Times*, 15 September 2001, 15(A), and John F. Harris, *Washington Post*, 14 September 2001, 3(C).

8. Cooperman reports that "The Justice Department's Civil Rights Division lists nine killings across the country as 'possible hate crimes' in revenge for the terrorist attacks." Nonlethal attacks on people and property were far more numerous. See Alan Cooperman, "Sept. 11 Backlash Murders and the State of Hate," *Washington Post*, 20 January 2002, 3(A) and 14(A).

9. Stephan G Bloom, *Postville: A Clash of Cultures in Heartland America* (New York: Harcourt, 2000).

10. Richard Bernstein, "Hassidim and Iowa Townsfolk: A Test of Diversity" in a review of Bloom, *New York Times*, 1 November 2000, B45.

11. Monique Deveaux, *Cultural Pluralism and Dilemmas of Justice* (Ithaca, N.Y.: Cornell University Press, 2000).

12. Nathan Glazer, *We Are All Multiculturalists Now* (Cambridge, Mass.: Harvard University Press, 1997), 118.

13. Chaim I. Waxman, "Is the Cup Half-Full or Half-Empty? Perspectives on the Future of the American Jewish Community," *American Pluralism and the Jewish Community*, ed. Seymour Martin Lipset (New Brunswick, N.J.: Transaction Publishers, 1990), 83, n.6.

14. Vasilikie Demos, "The Production of Ethnicity among Greek Kytherian Women in Australia" (paper presented at the annual meeting of the North Central Sociological Association, Fort Wayne, Indiana, April 1992).

15. Samuel Oliner and Pearl M. Oliner, *The Altruistic Personality: Rescuers of Jews in Nazi Europe* (New York: The Free Press, 1988). I learned about the Oliners' work through a review of two other books by Robert Kanigel, "The Better Angels of Our Nature," *Washington Post, Book World*, 27 May 1990. The two books reviewed by Kanigel are Morton Hunt, *The Compassionate Beast: What Science Is Discovering about the*

Humane Side of Humankind (New York: Morrow, 1990) and Alfie Kohn, *The Brighter Side of Human Nature: Altruism and Empathy in Everyday Life* (New York: Basic Books, 1990).

16. Evidence for this appears in Irwin Deutscher, Fred P. Pestello and H. Frances G. Pestello, *Sentiments and Acts* (New York: Aldine de Gruyter, 1993).

17. Kanigel, "The Better Angels."

18. Daniel Williams, "Three Kosovo Men Extinguish the Flames of Ethnic Hatred," *Washington Post*, 15 June 1999, 25(A) and 28(A).

19. Stanley Milgram, "Nationality and Conformity," *Scientific American*, 205 (1961): 45-51 (1961); "Group Pressure And Action against a Person," *Journal of Abnormal and Social Psychology* 69 (1964): 137-43; "Some Conditions of Obedience and Disobedience to Authority," *International Journal of Psychiatry* 6 (1968): 59-76.

20. Irwin Deutscher, *What We Say/What We Do* (Glenview, Ill.: Scott, Foresman & Company, 1973), 236-40.

21. David Riesman, et al., *The Lonely Crowd* (New Haven: Yale, Conn., University Press, 1951).

22. Shmuel Eisenstadt, "The American Jewish Experience and American Pluralism," in *American Pluralism*, 43.

23. Arnold Eisen, "The Rhetoric of Chosenness and the Fabrication of American Jewish Identity," in *American Pluralism*, 66. Biblical sources are II Kings 23: 27, Psalms 78: 67-68, and Isaiah 7: 15 and 41: 18.

24. Quoted by Eisen, "The Rhetoric of Chosenness," 53. The quotation is from Arthur Hertzberg, "The Condition of Jewish Belief" [reprinted from *Commentary* (August 1966)] in *Being Jewish in America* (New York: Schocken, 1979), 20.

25. Brewer, *Anti-Catholicism*, 135-38.

26. Meg Greenfield, "The Trouble with Tribes," *Washington Post*, 20 July 1998, 17(A).

27. Mary Kay Magistad, "Cambodian Violence against Ethnic Vietnamese Said to Flourish," *Washington Post*, 5 December 1992, 20 (A).

28. Michael A. Fletcher, "The Color of Controversy," *Washington Post*, 11 October 1997, 1-2(H). Fletcher interviewed Stephan and Abigail Thernstrom and they call their book *America in Black and White: One Nation Indivisible*. Fletcher says it is an optimistic tome, employing statistical evidence to describe black progress and improving racial attitudes in America.

29. I am grateful to Jay Weinstein for permitting me to bounce these concerns off of him and for his encouragement and help in dealing with them.Weinstein organized and chaired a session at the World Congress of the International Institute of Sociology in Tel Aviv, Israel (July, 1999) which provided an opportunity for me to air many of the ideas in this chapter.

30. Eugene Robinson, "Blending in or Wiping Out: Immigration Tests a European Society," *Washington Post*, 5 July 1998, 1(A) and 14(A).

31. Murray L. Wax, "How Culture Misdirects Multiculturalism," *Anthropology and Education Quarterly* 24, no. 2 (1993

Index

About the Author

Irwin Deutscher is Professor Emeritus of Sociology at the University of Akron. He is author or coauthor of 6 books and over 100 articles. He is past president of the Society for the Study of Social Problems and the Society for Applied sociology. Among his many awards is the Distinguished Career award for the practice of sociology from the American Sociological Association. Deutscher holds four degrees from the University of Missouri and received a distinguished alumnus award from the College of Arts and Science at that institution. He has lectured in the United States, Europe, and Asia and holds the Annondale Memorial Medal for distinguished service to Indian Anthropology. He is a volunteer with Amnesty International serving as the Legislative Coordinator for Washington, D.C.

RECEIVED APR 2 9 2003

DATE DUE
